Ce livre appartient à :

_____

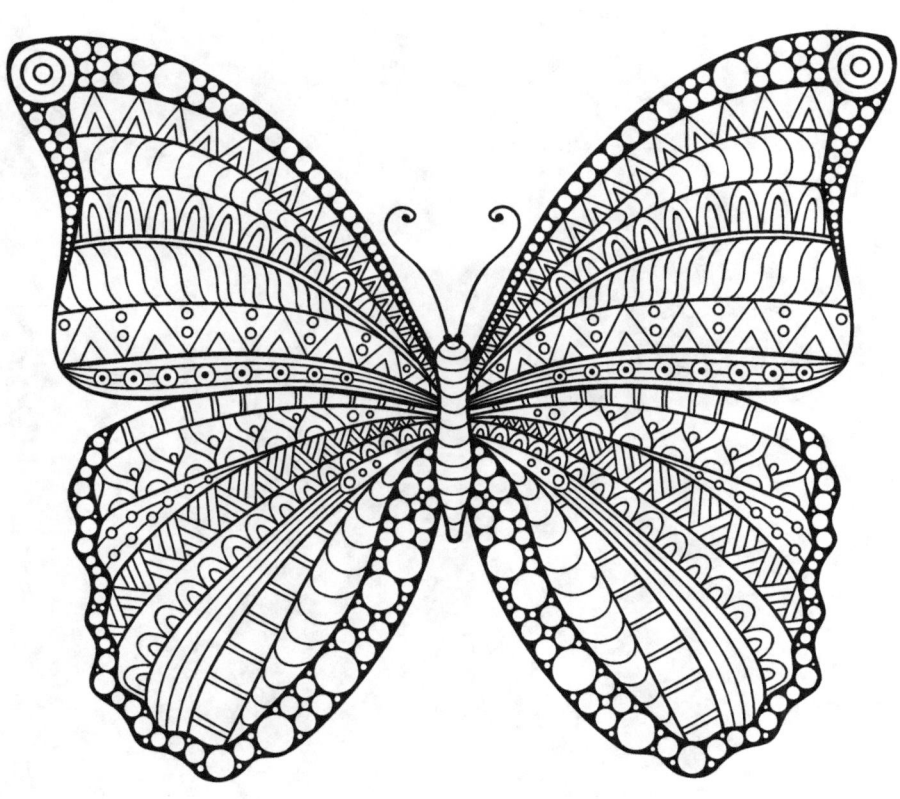

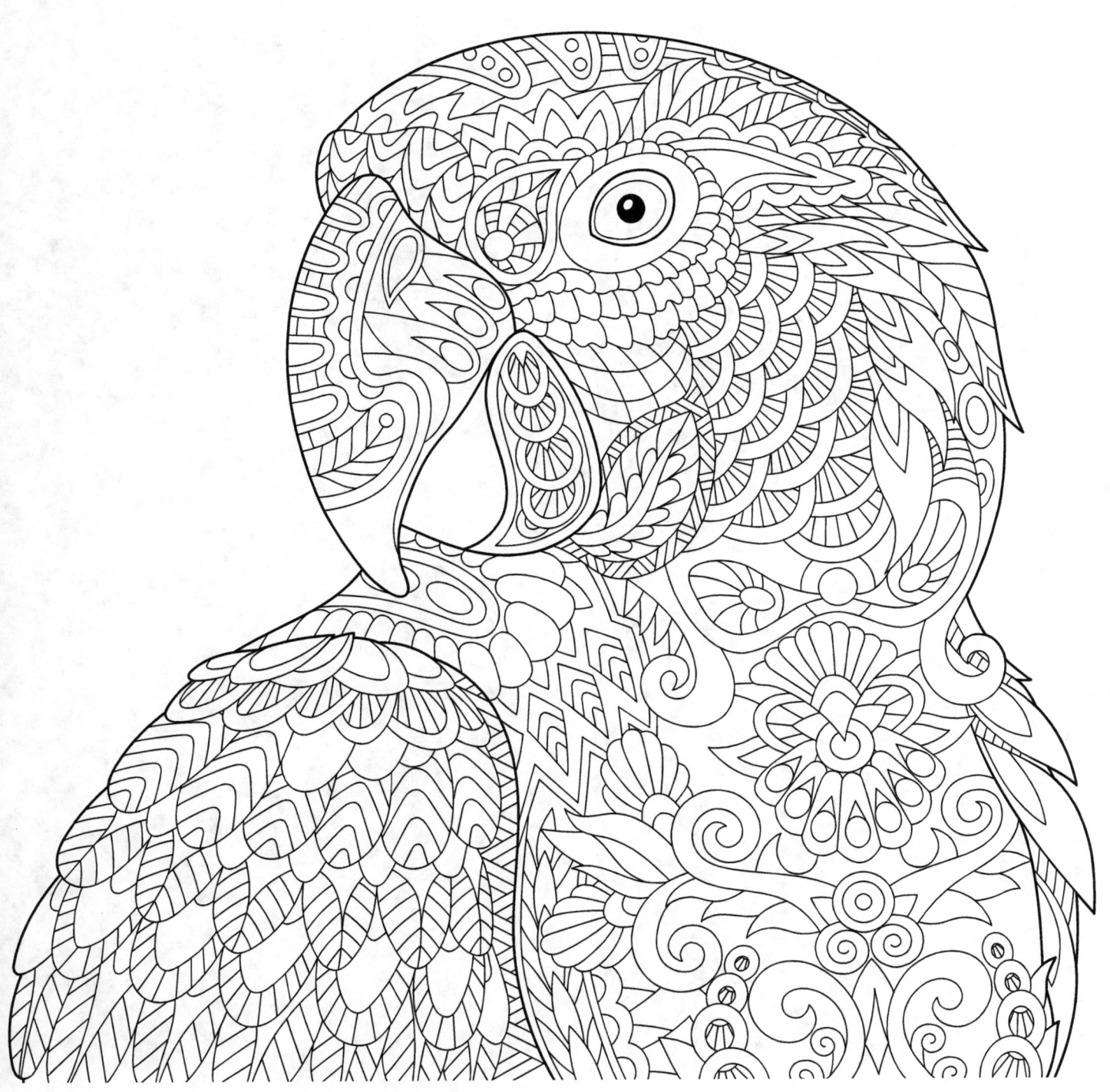

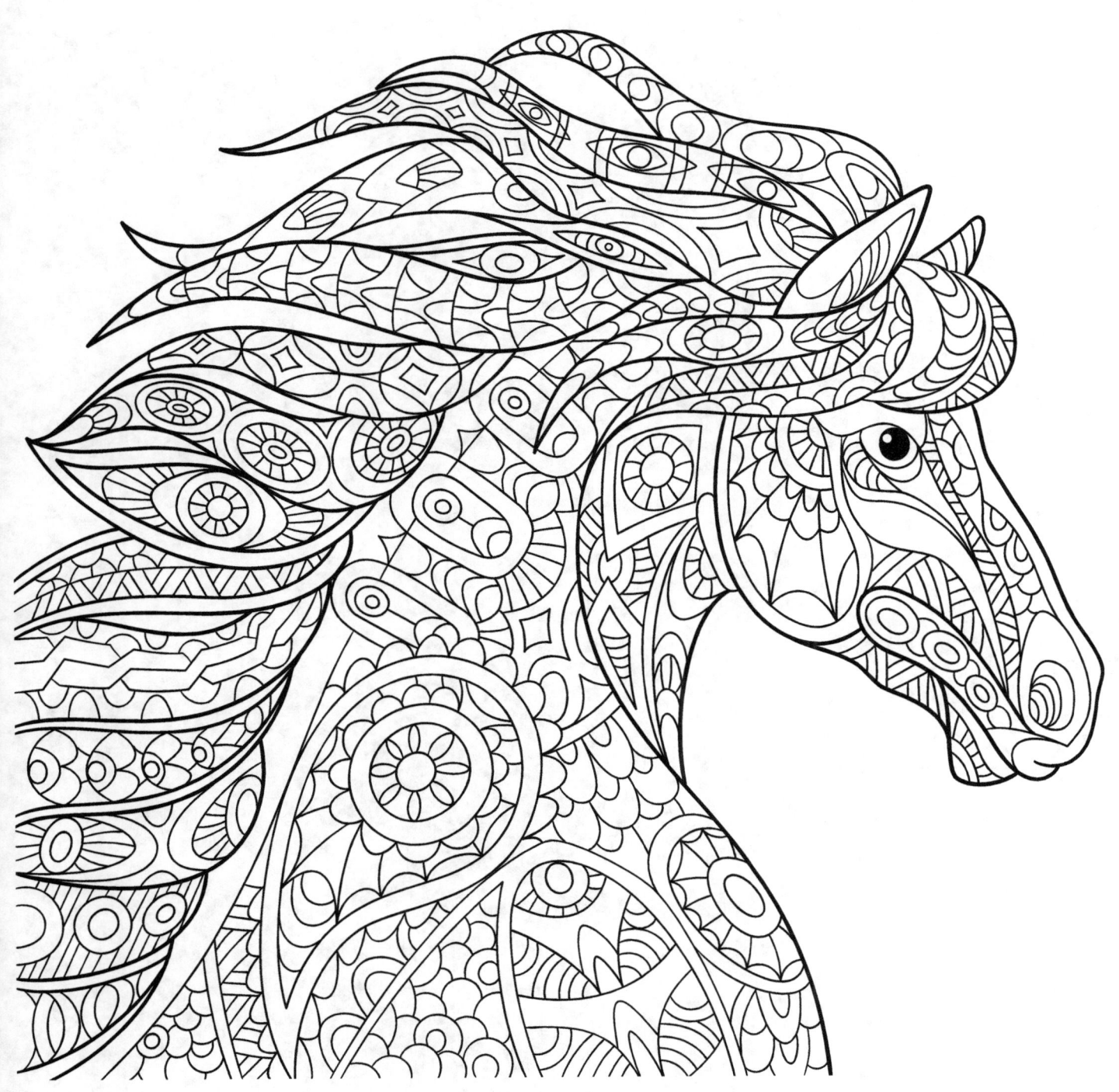

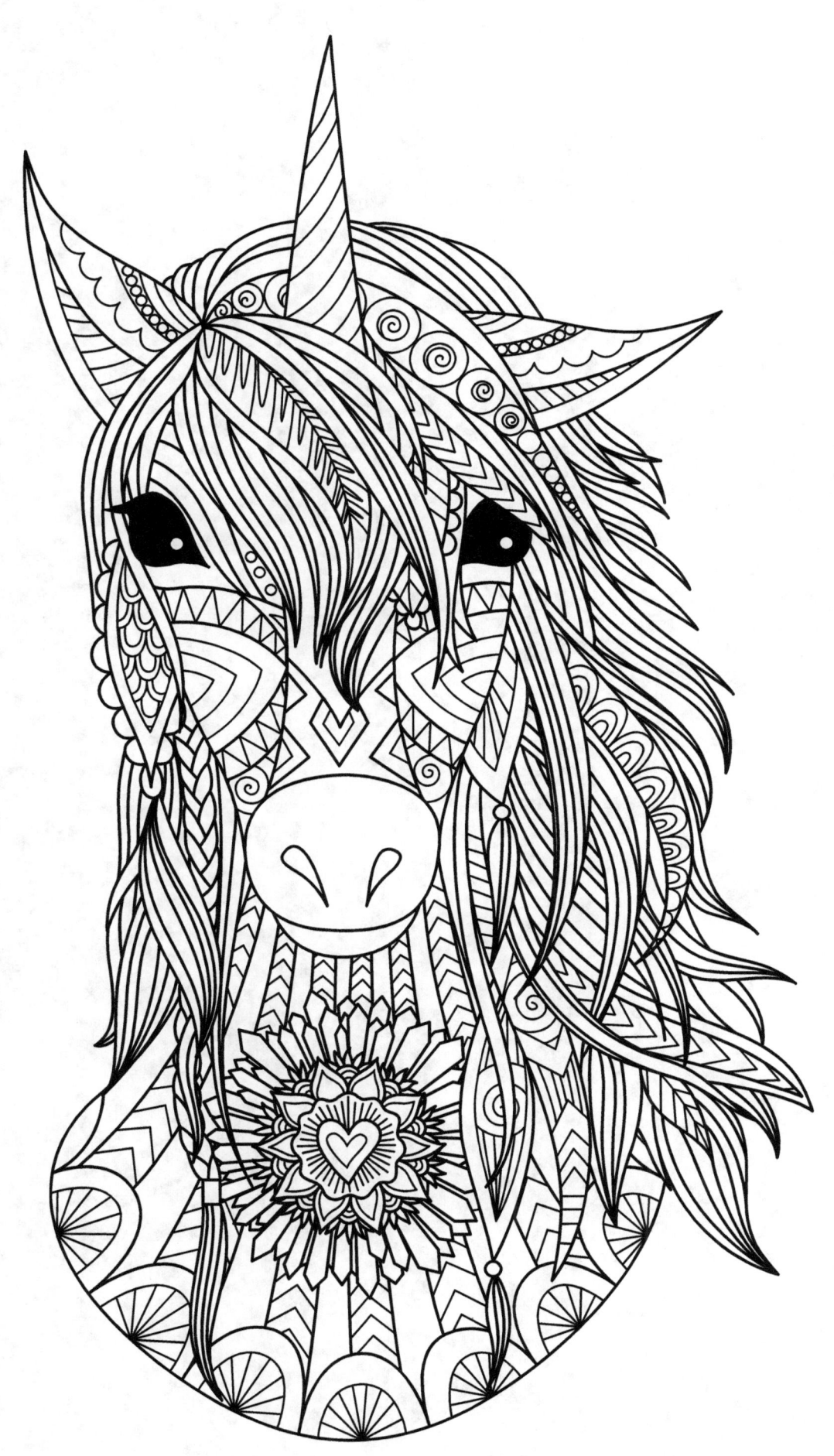

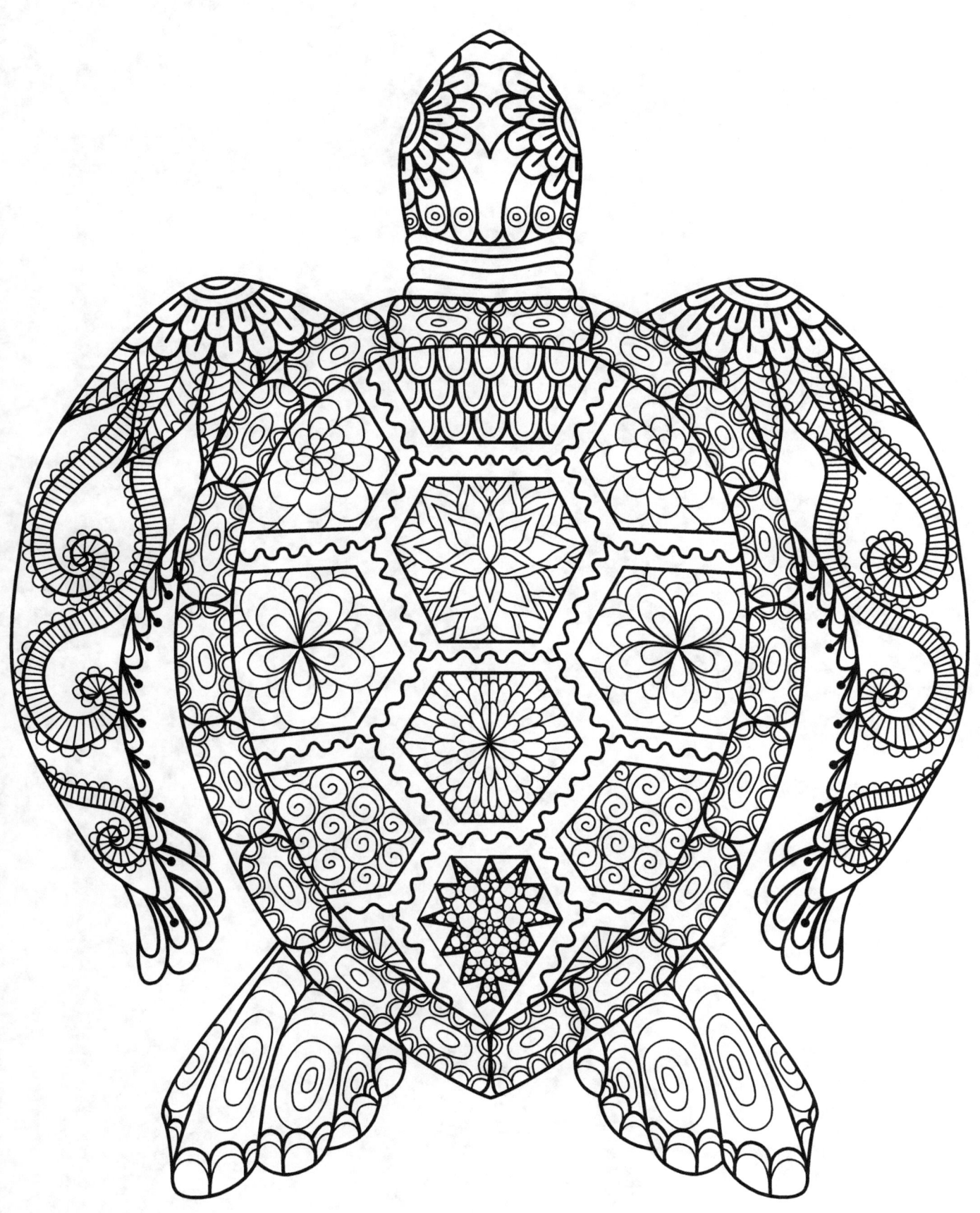

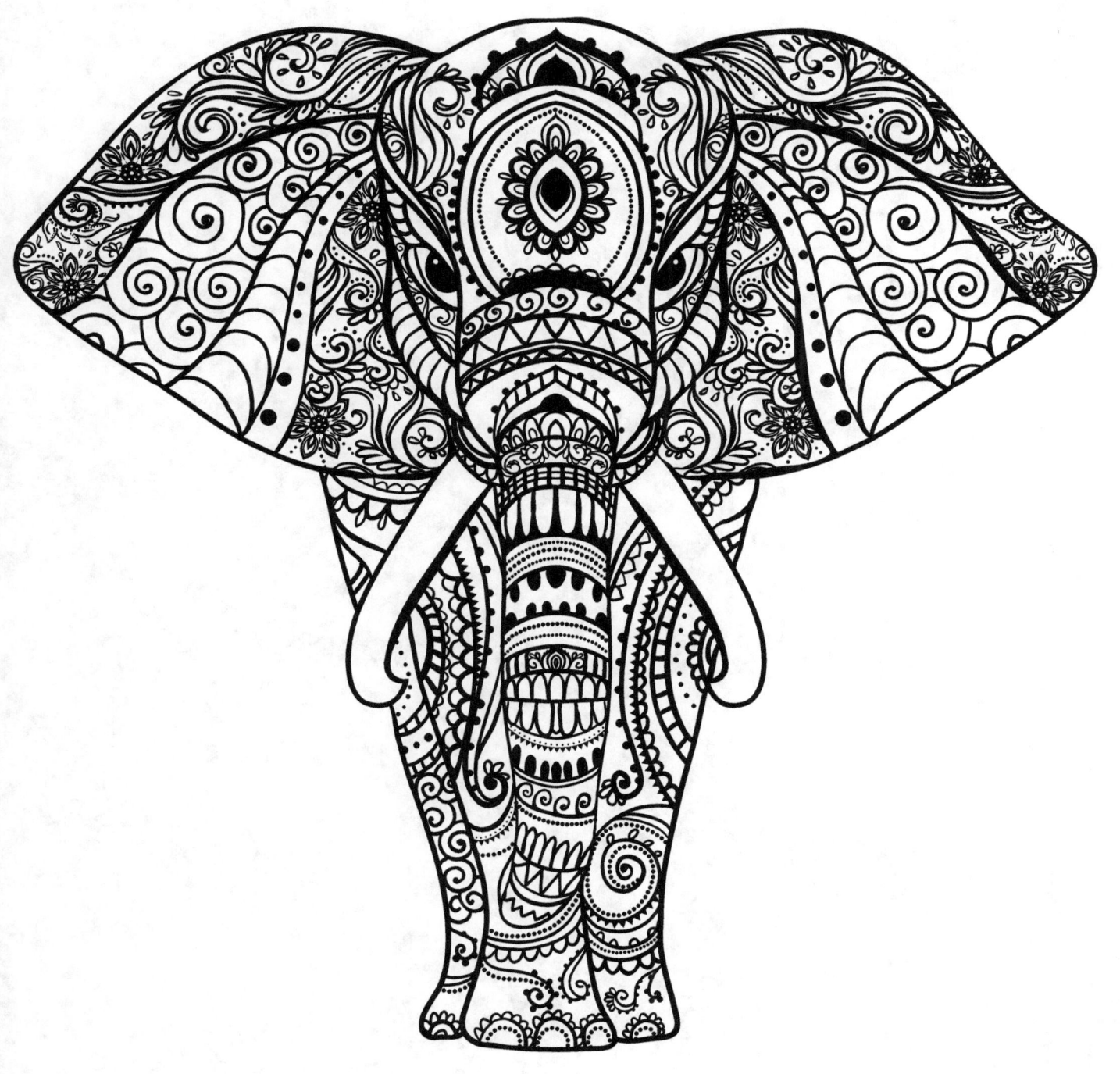

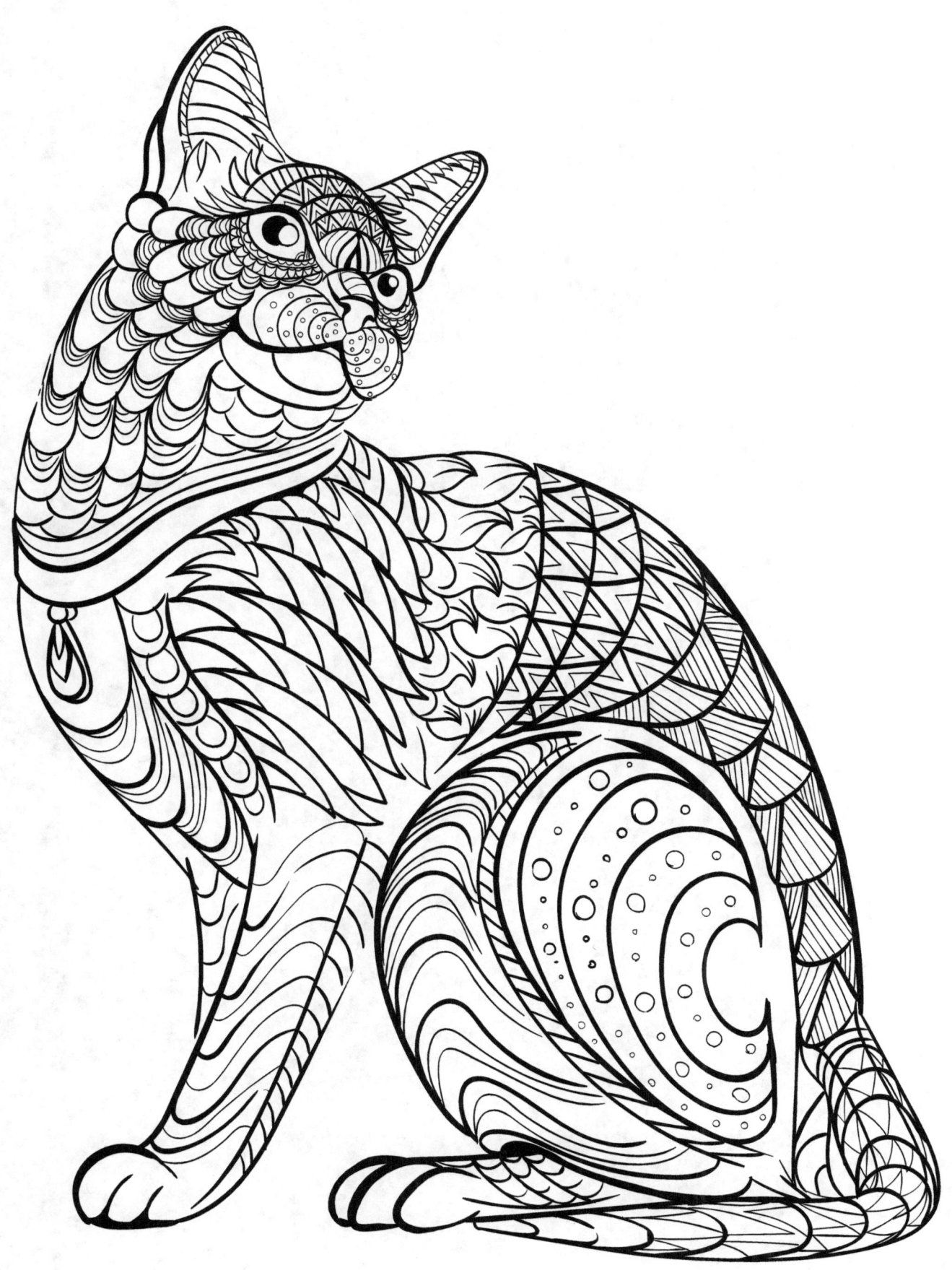

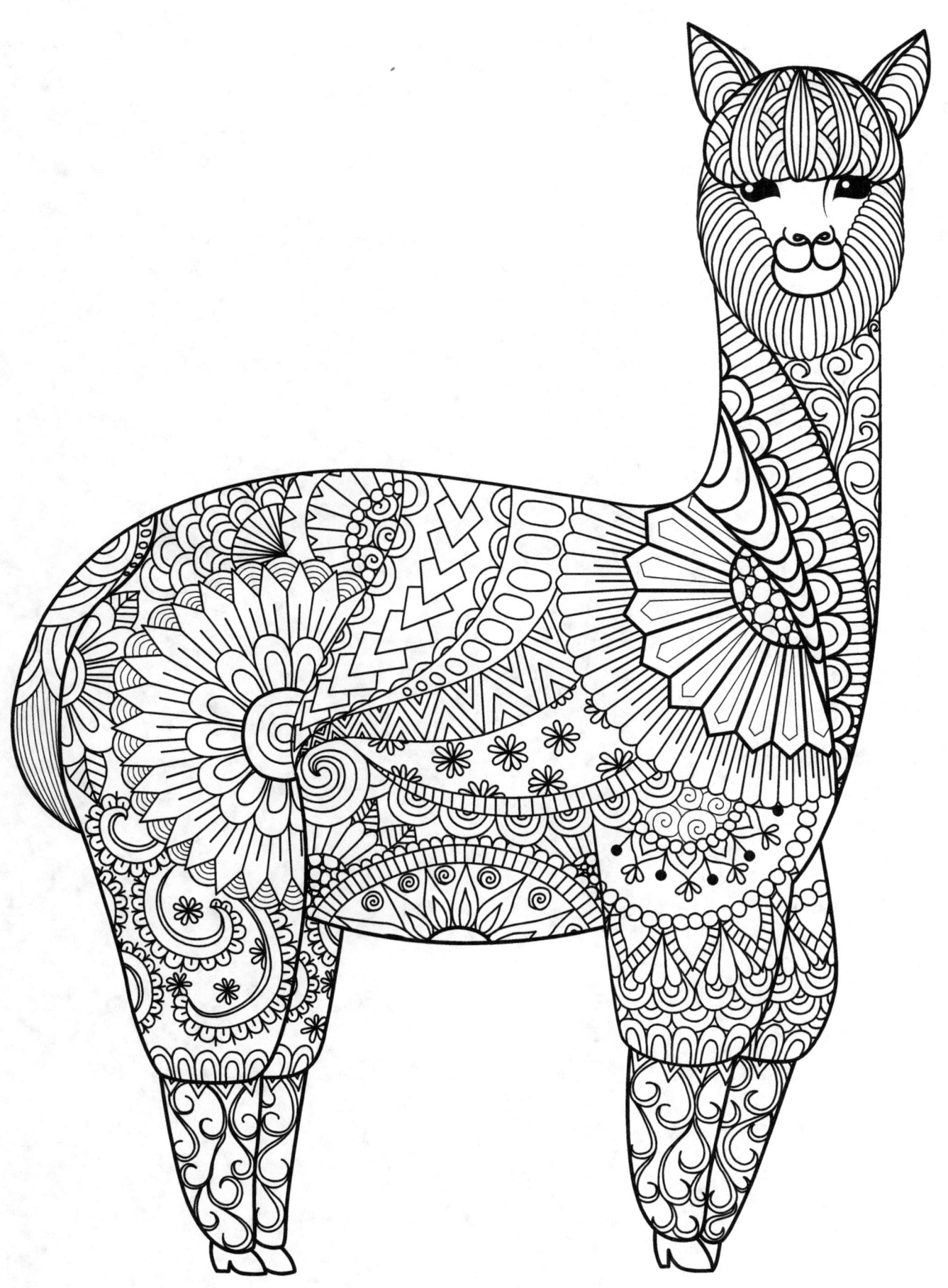

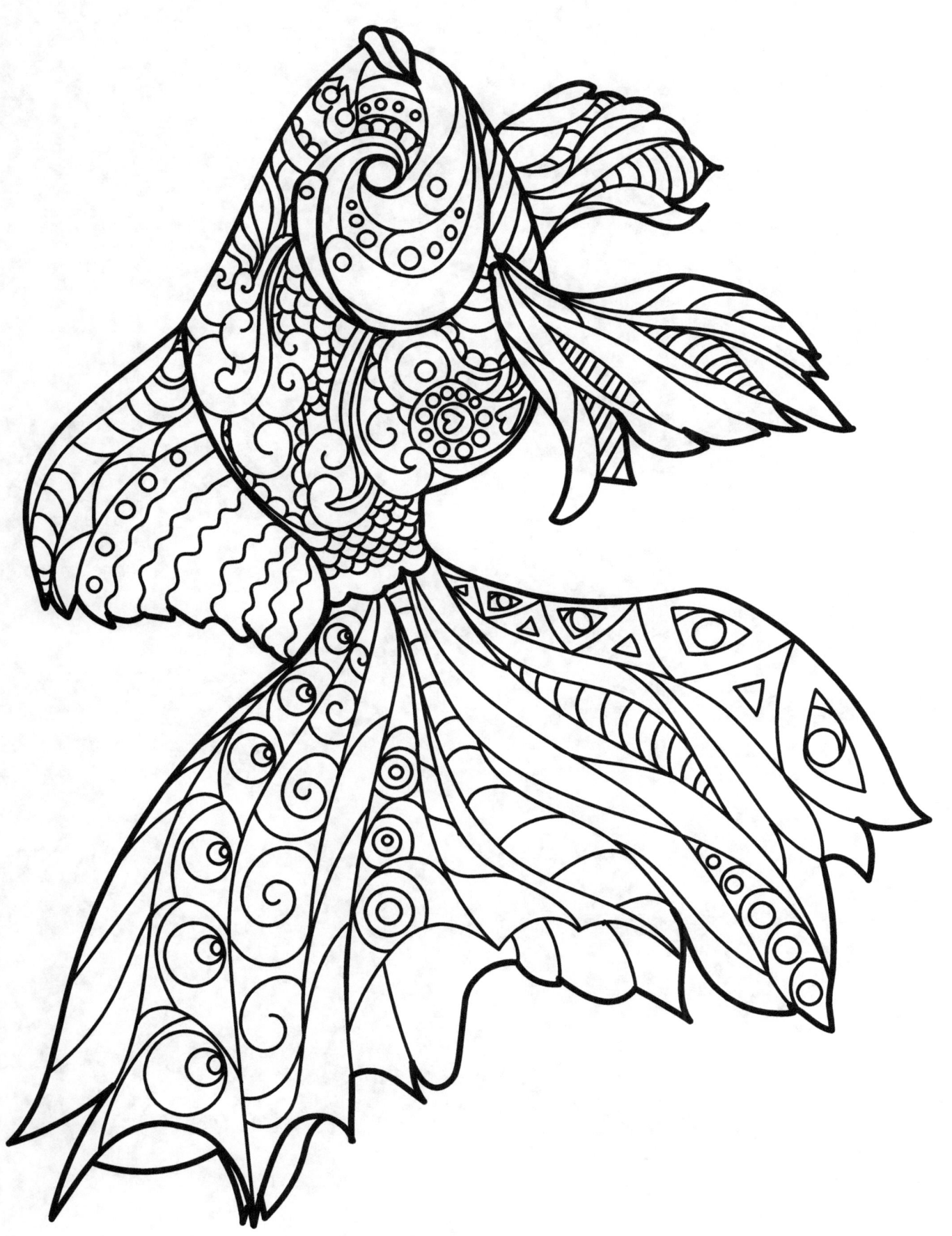

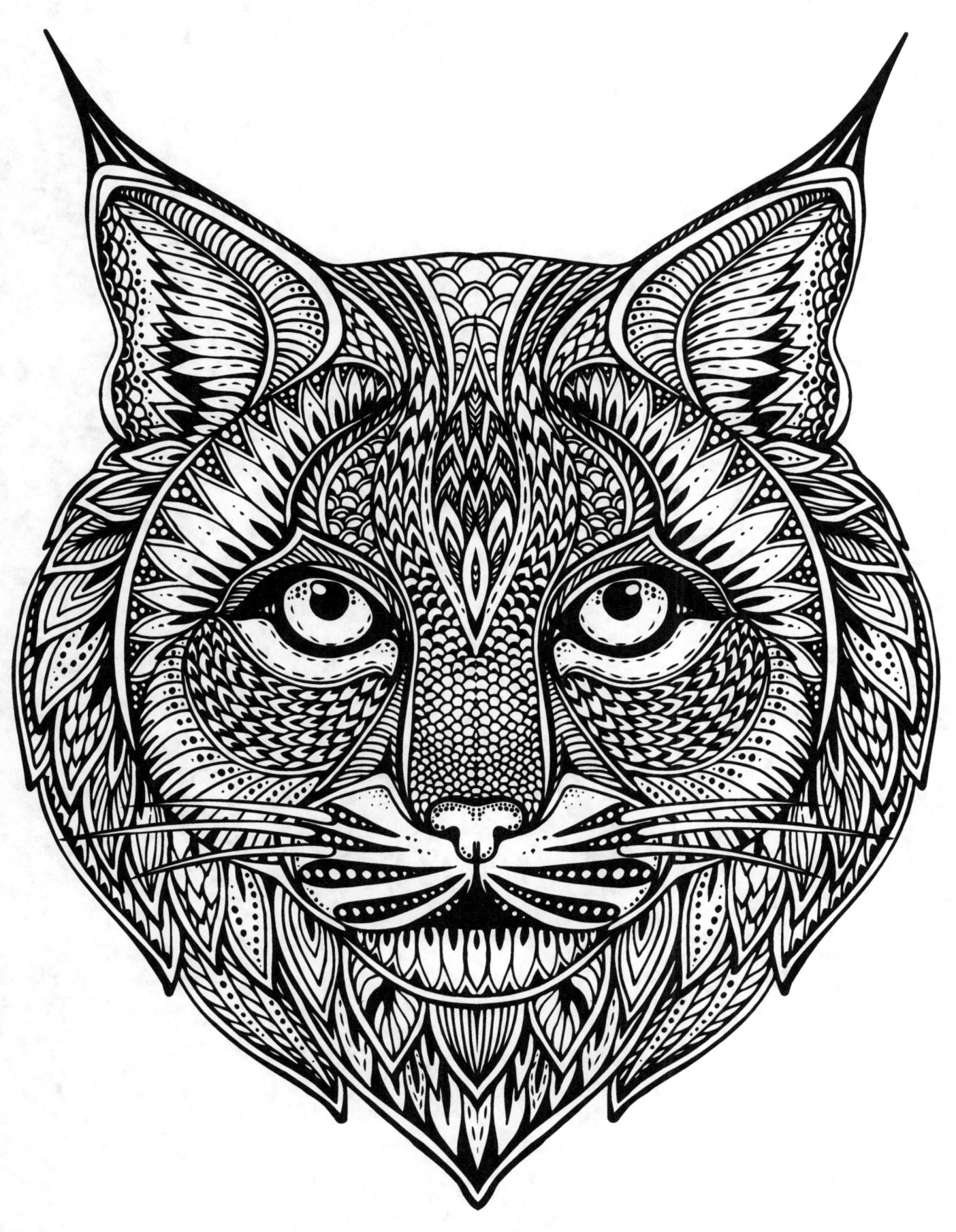

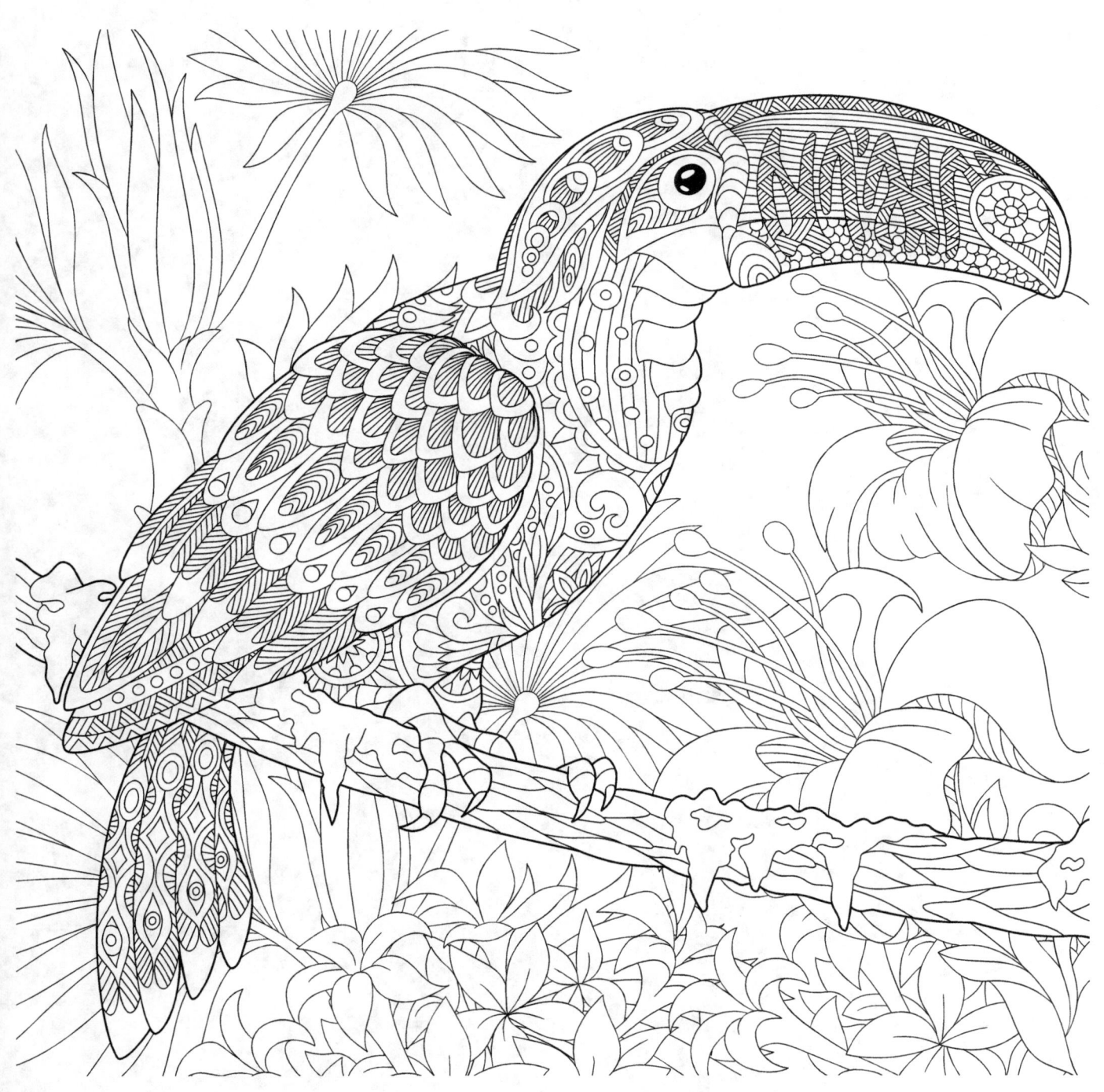

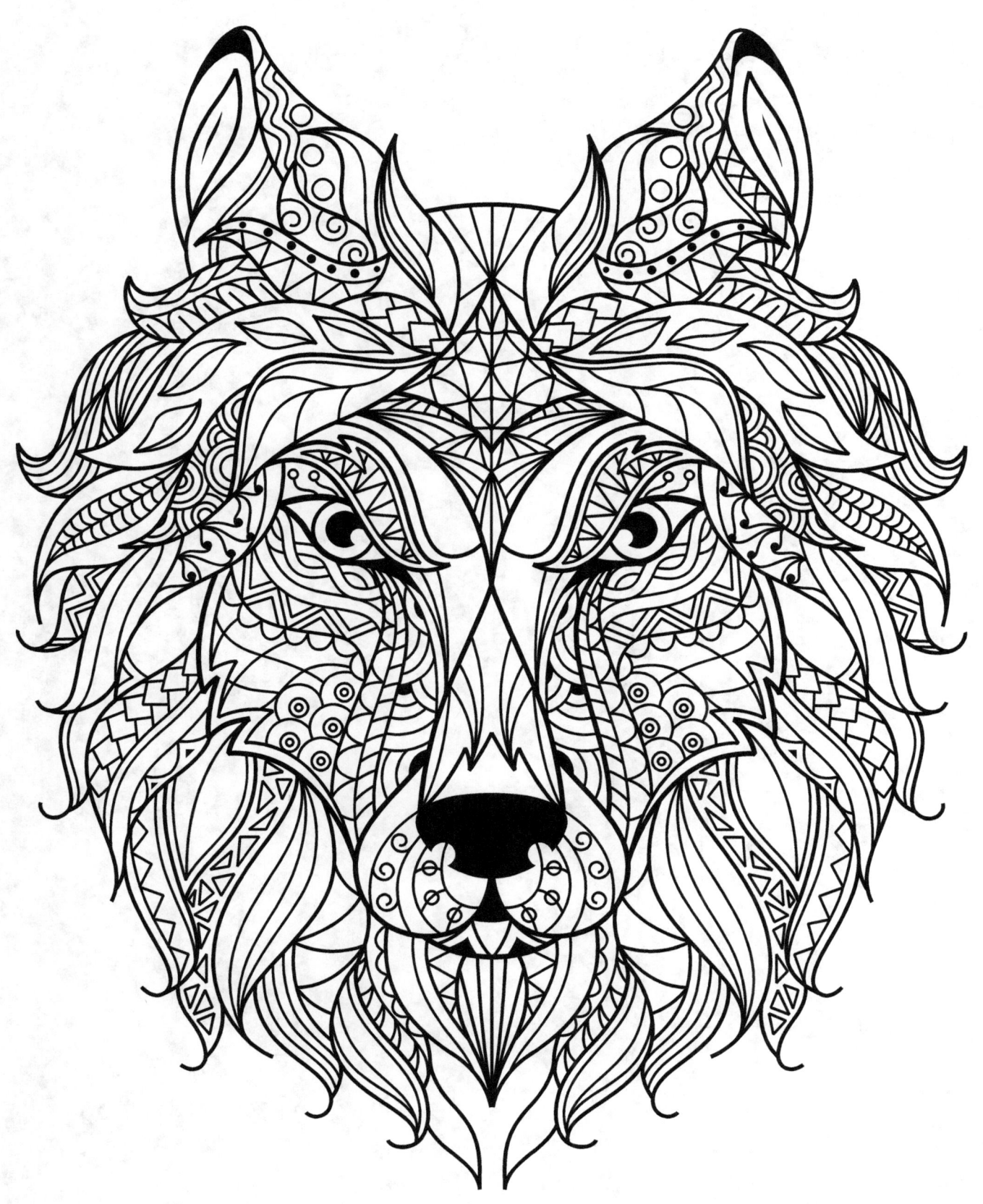

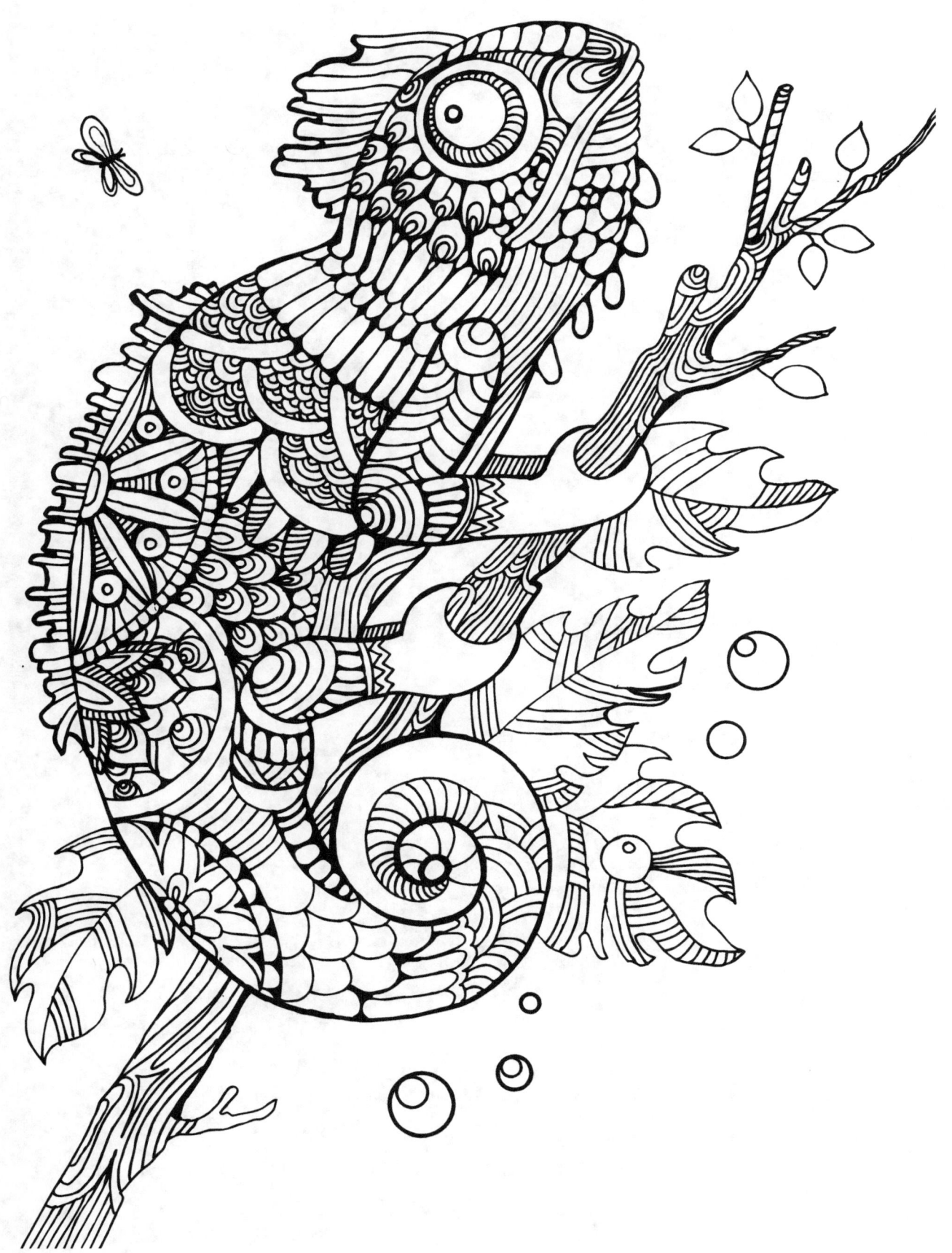

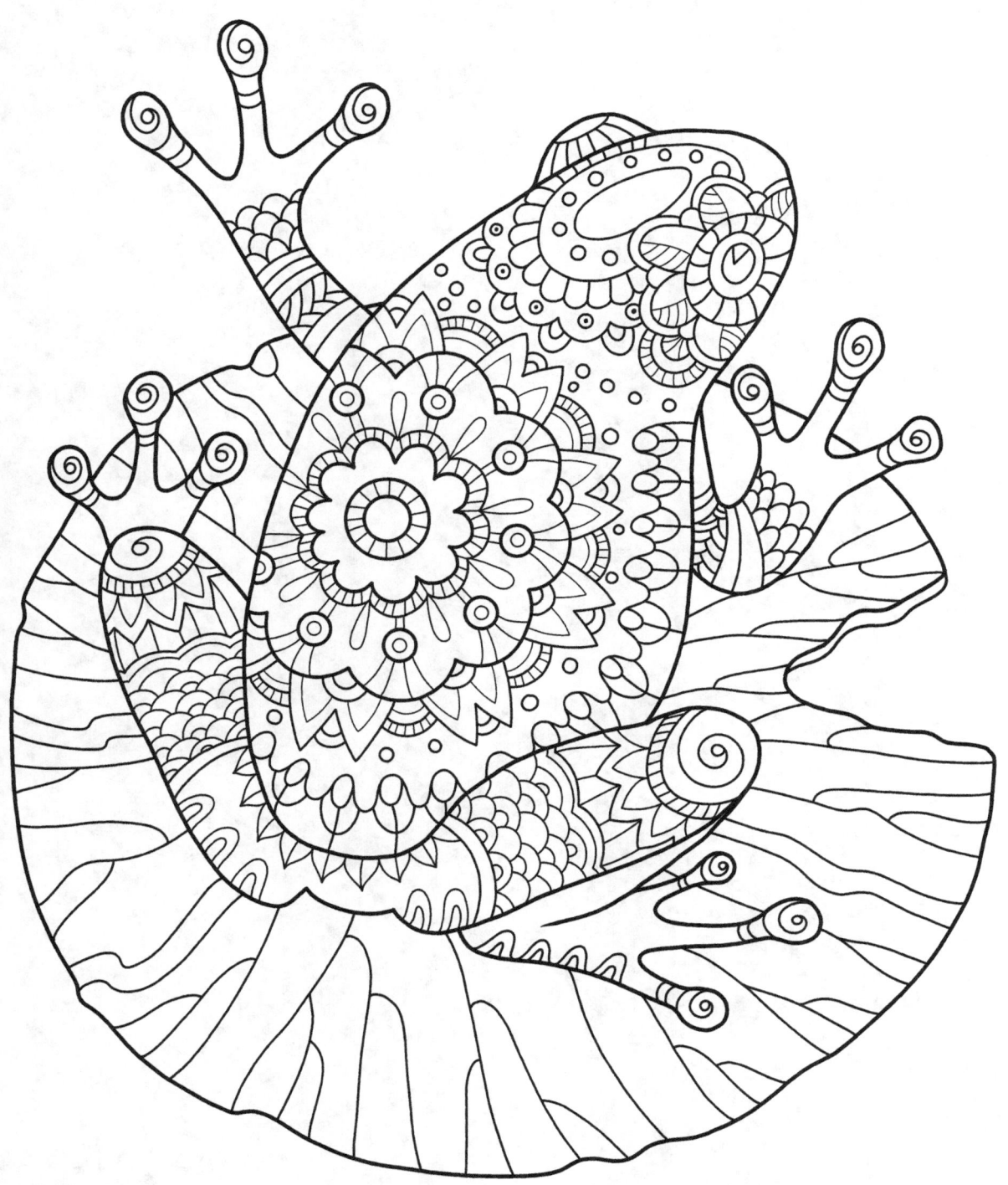

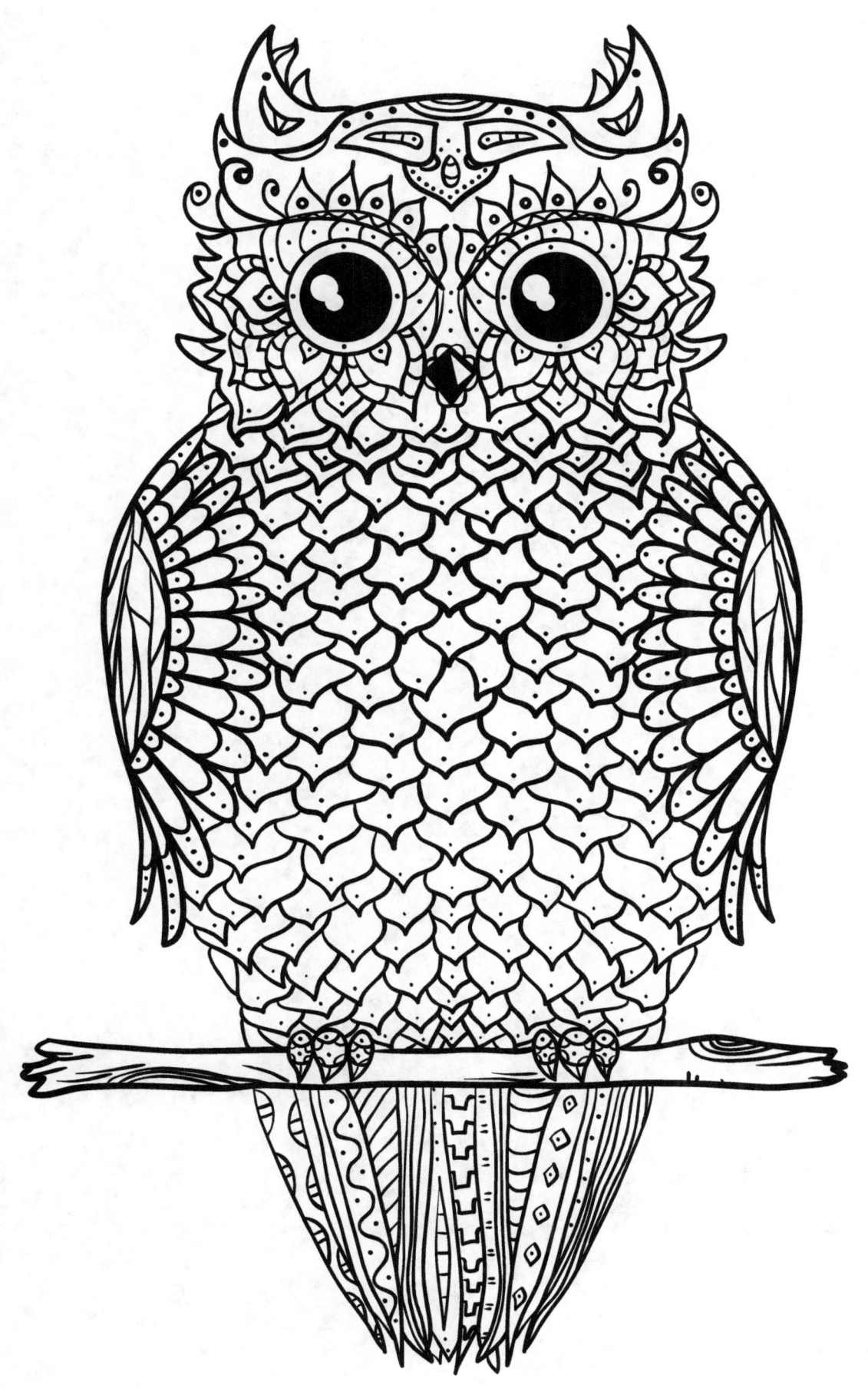

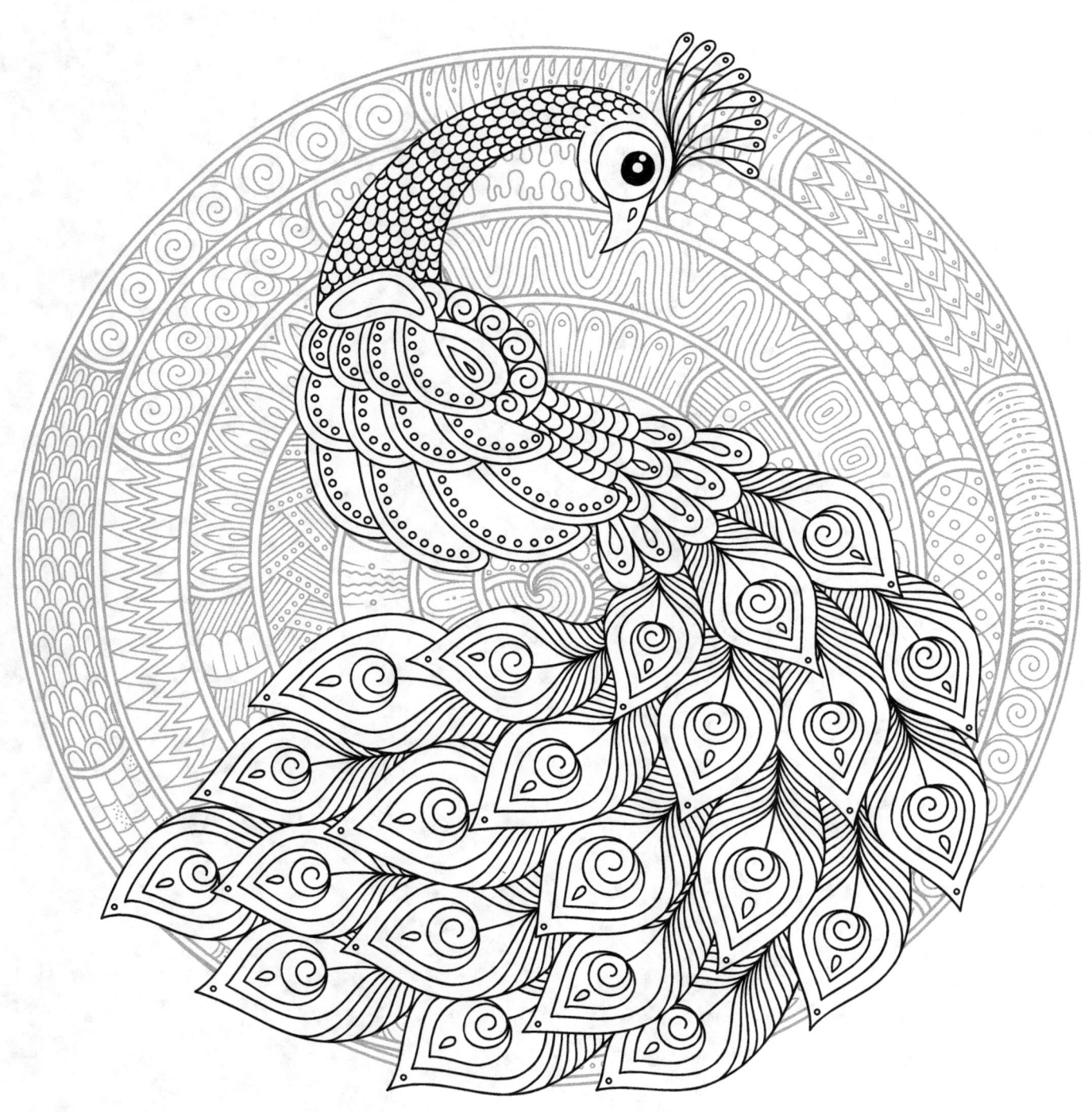

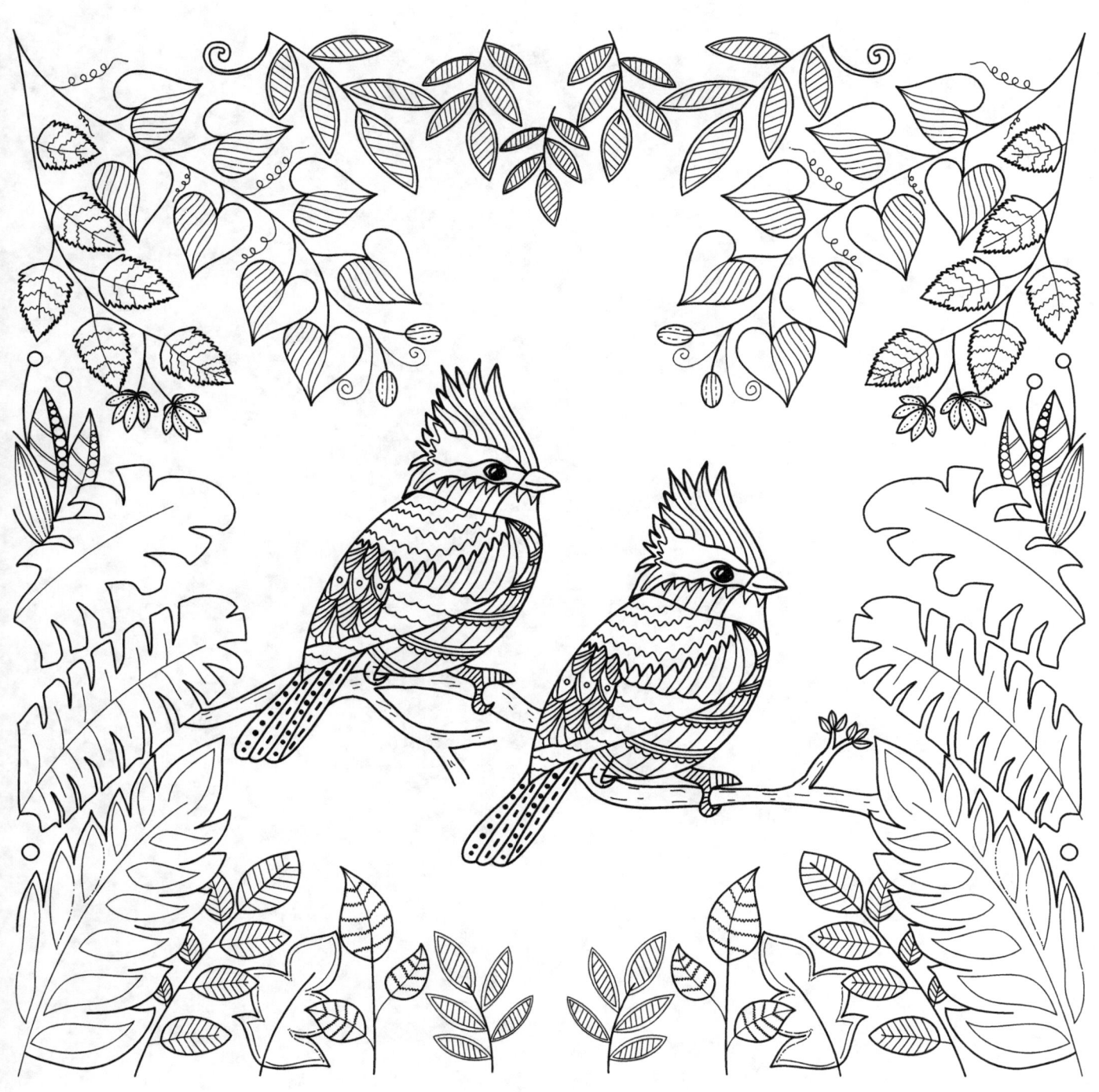

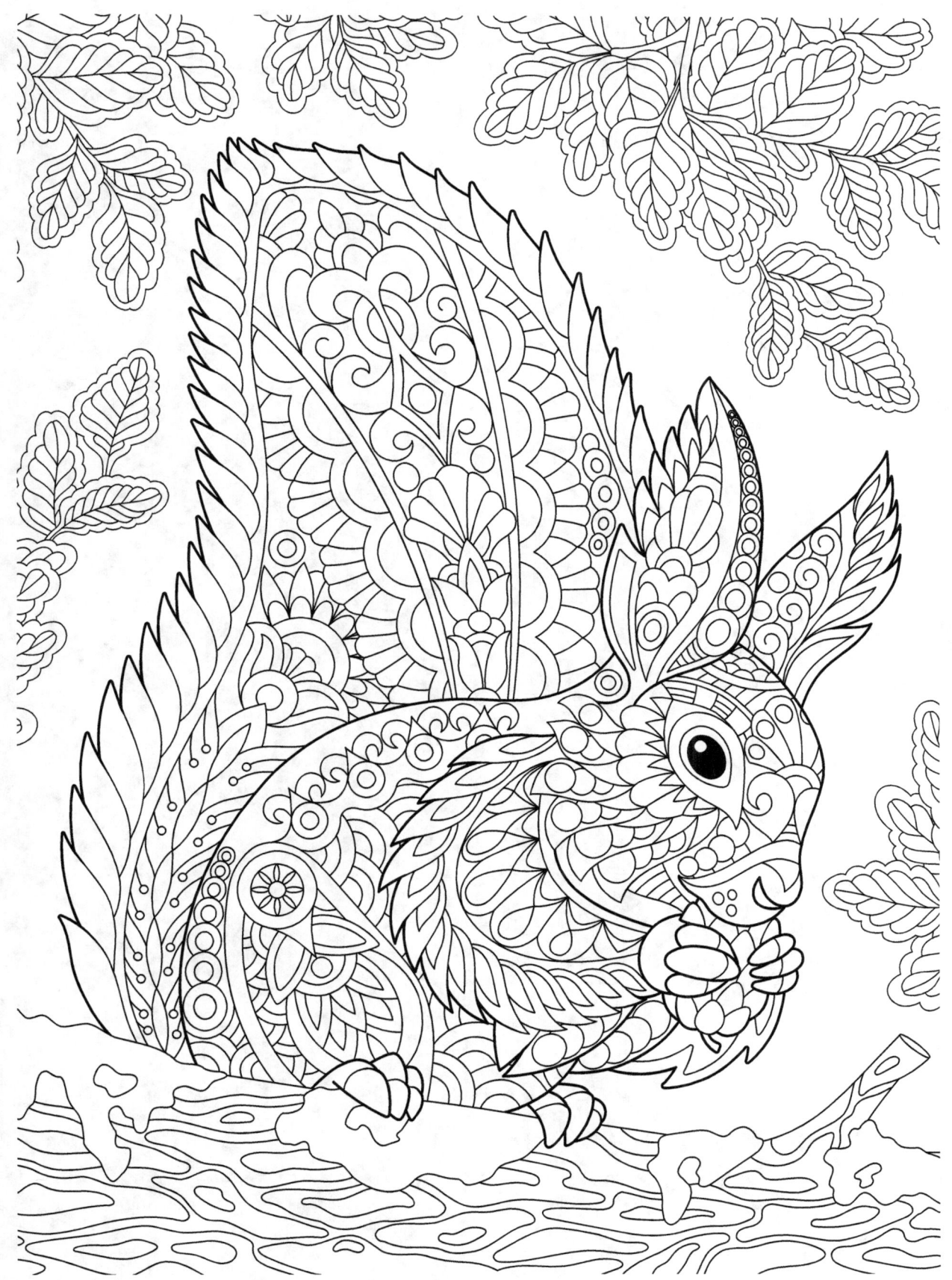

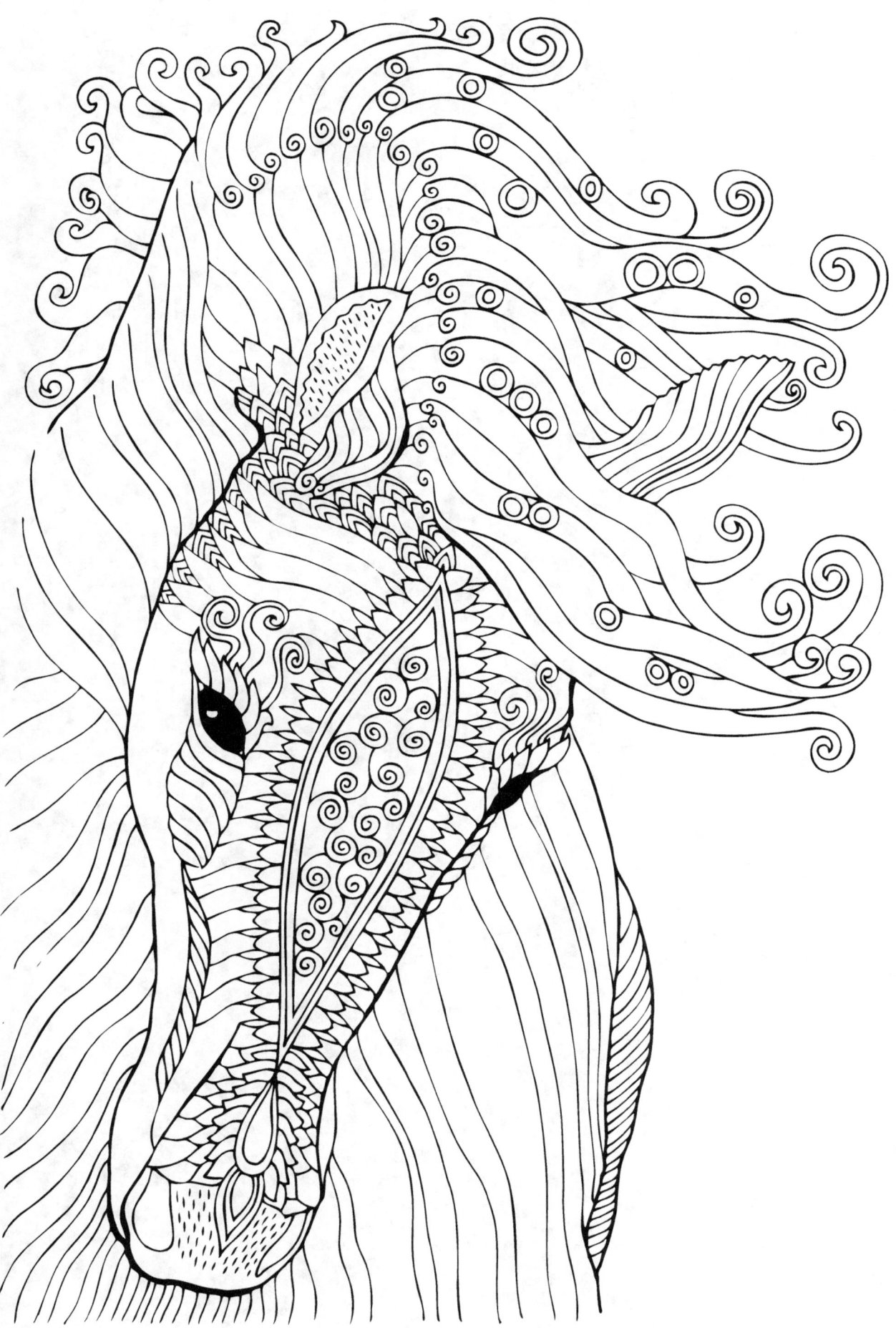

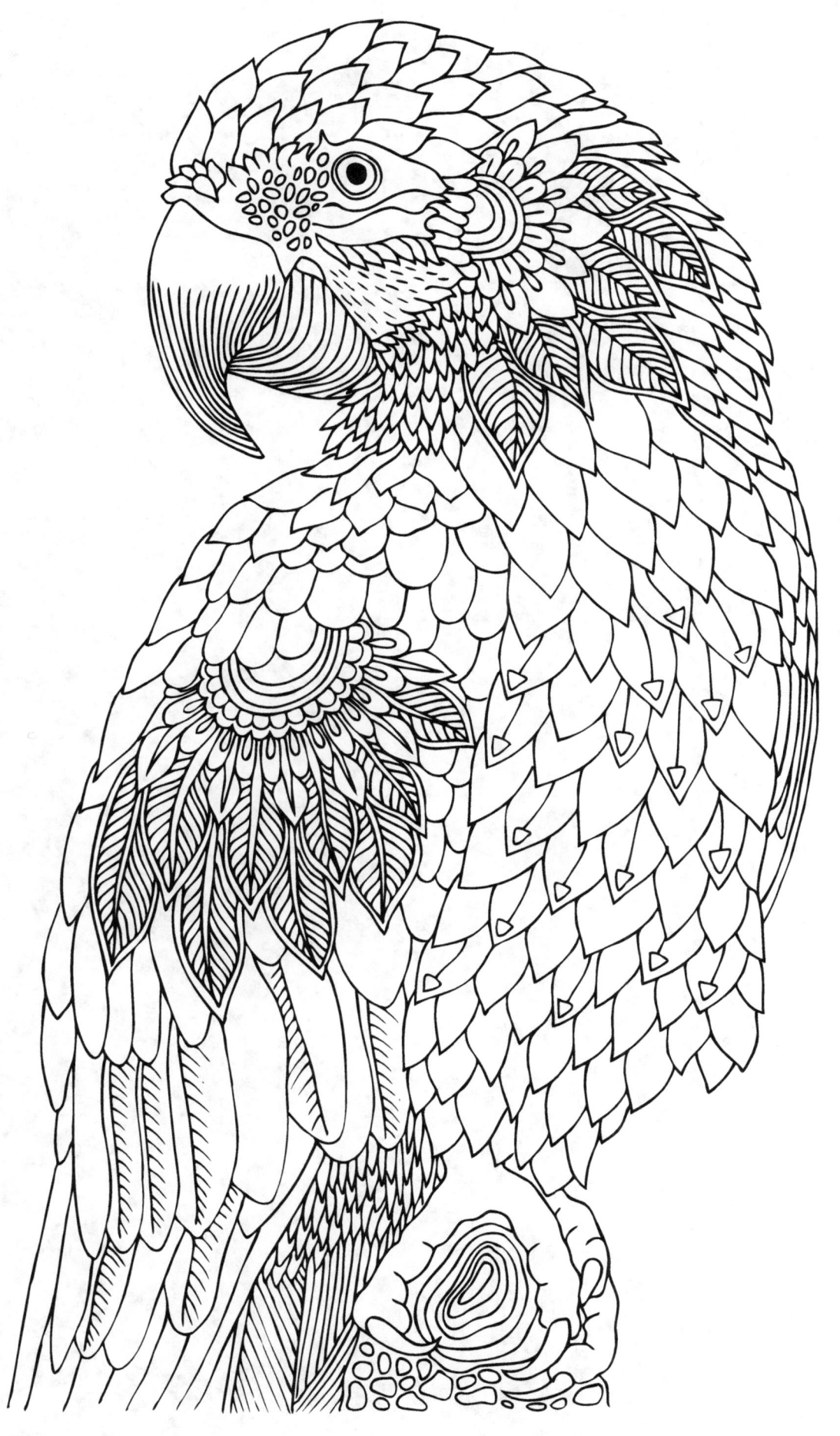

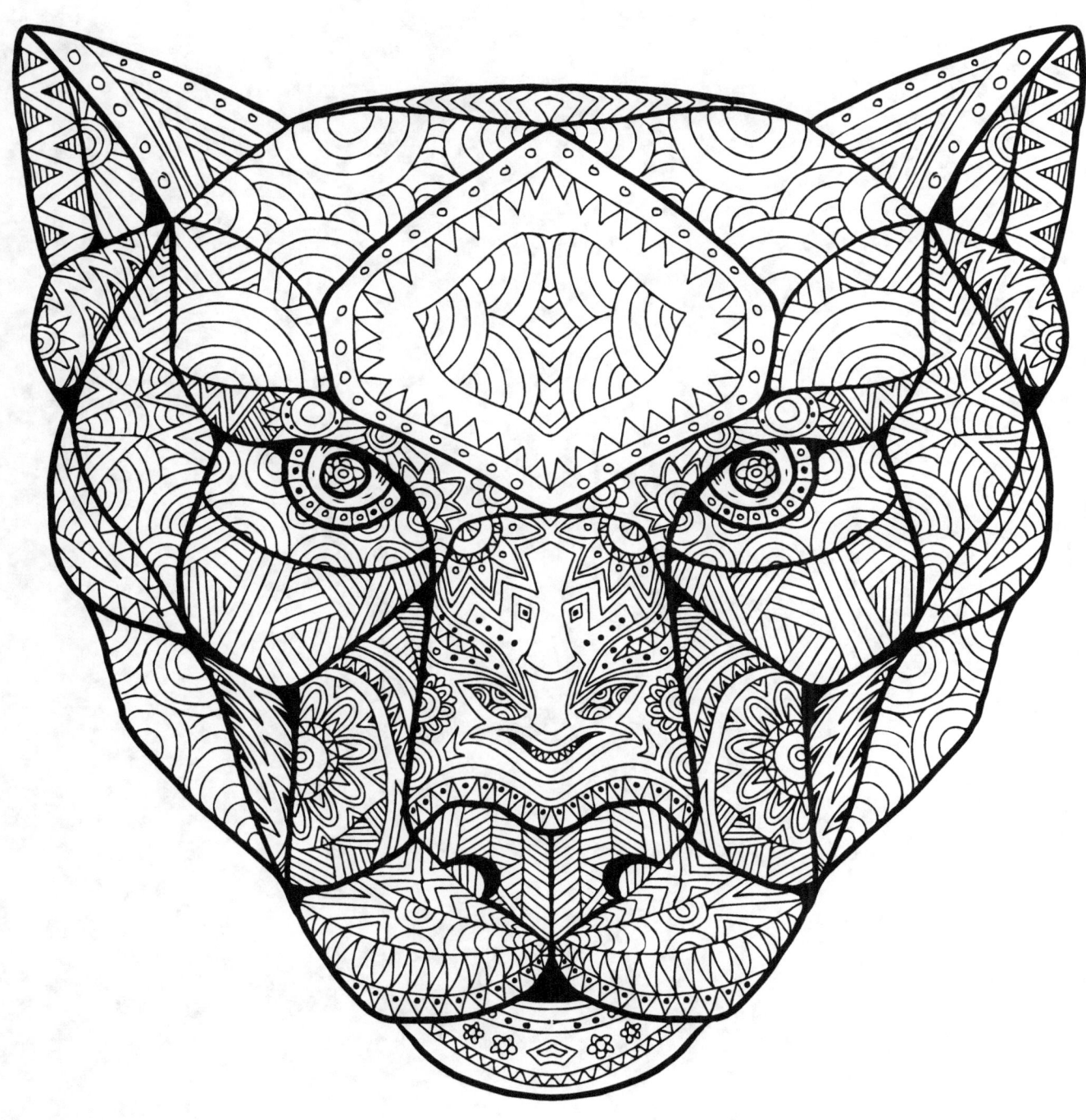

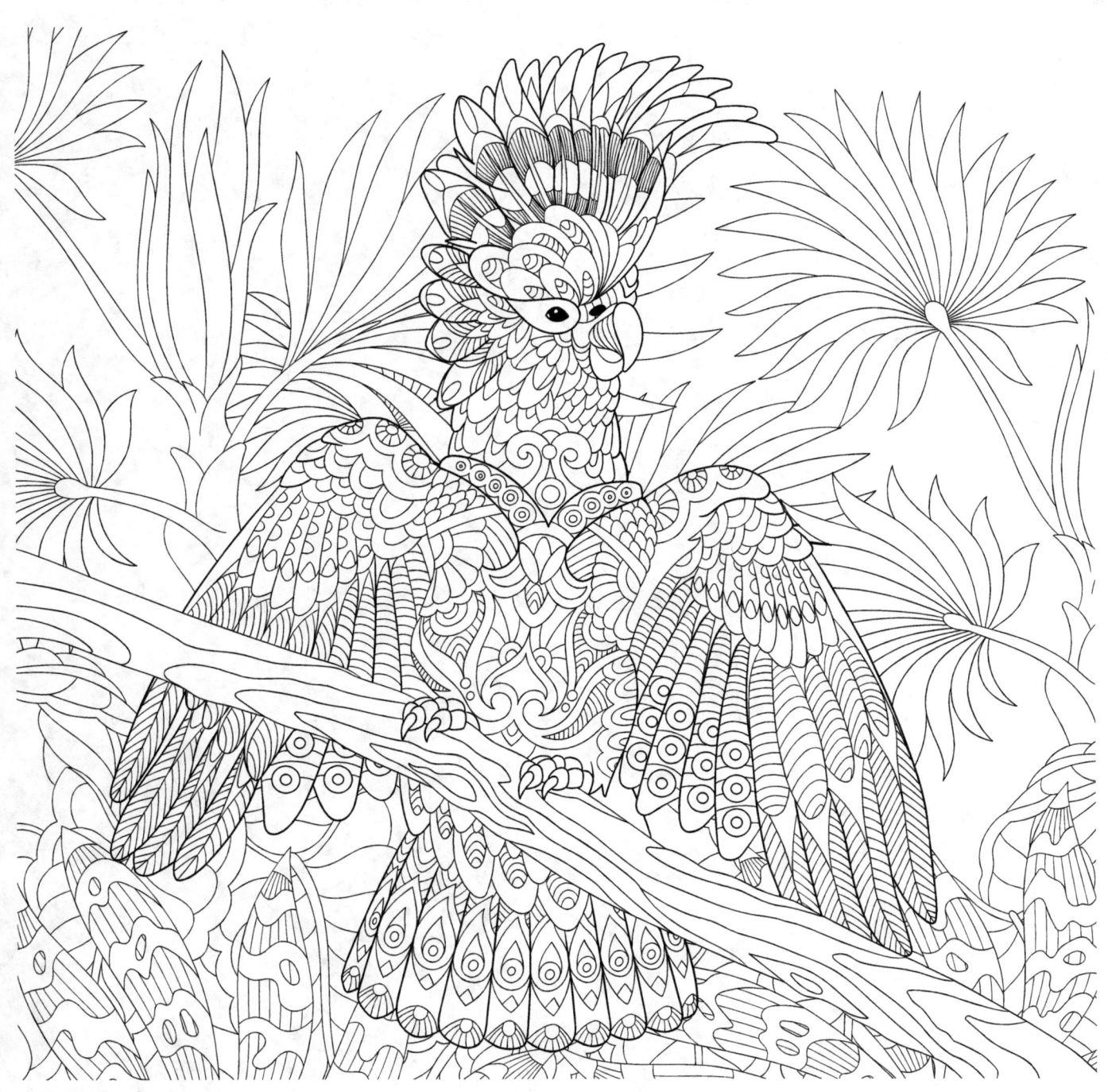

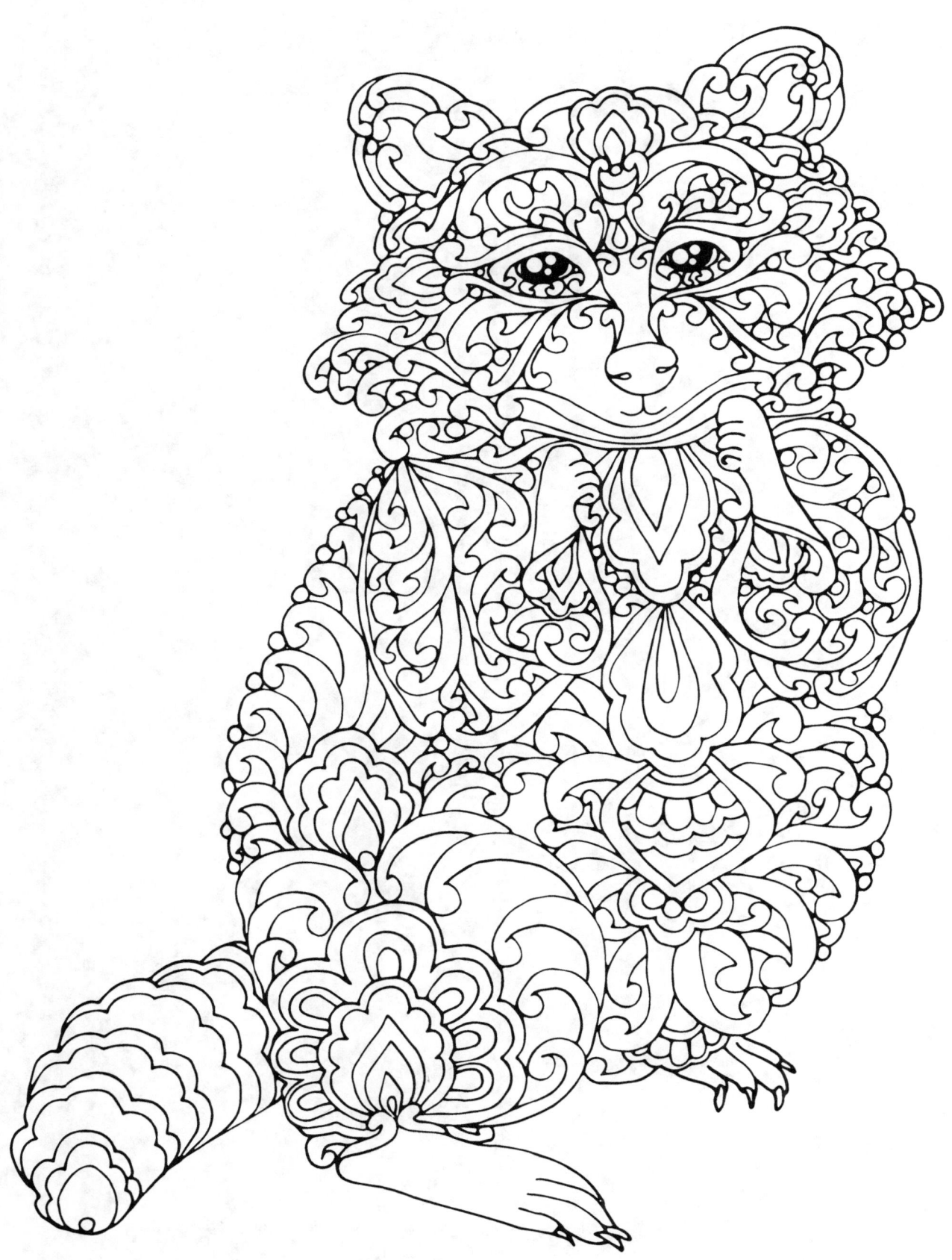

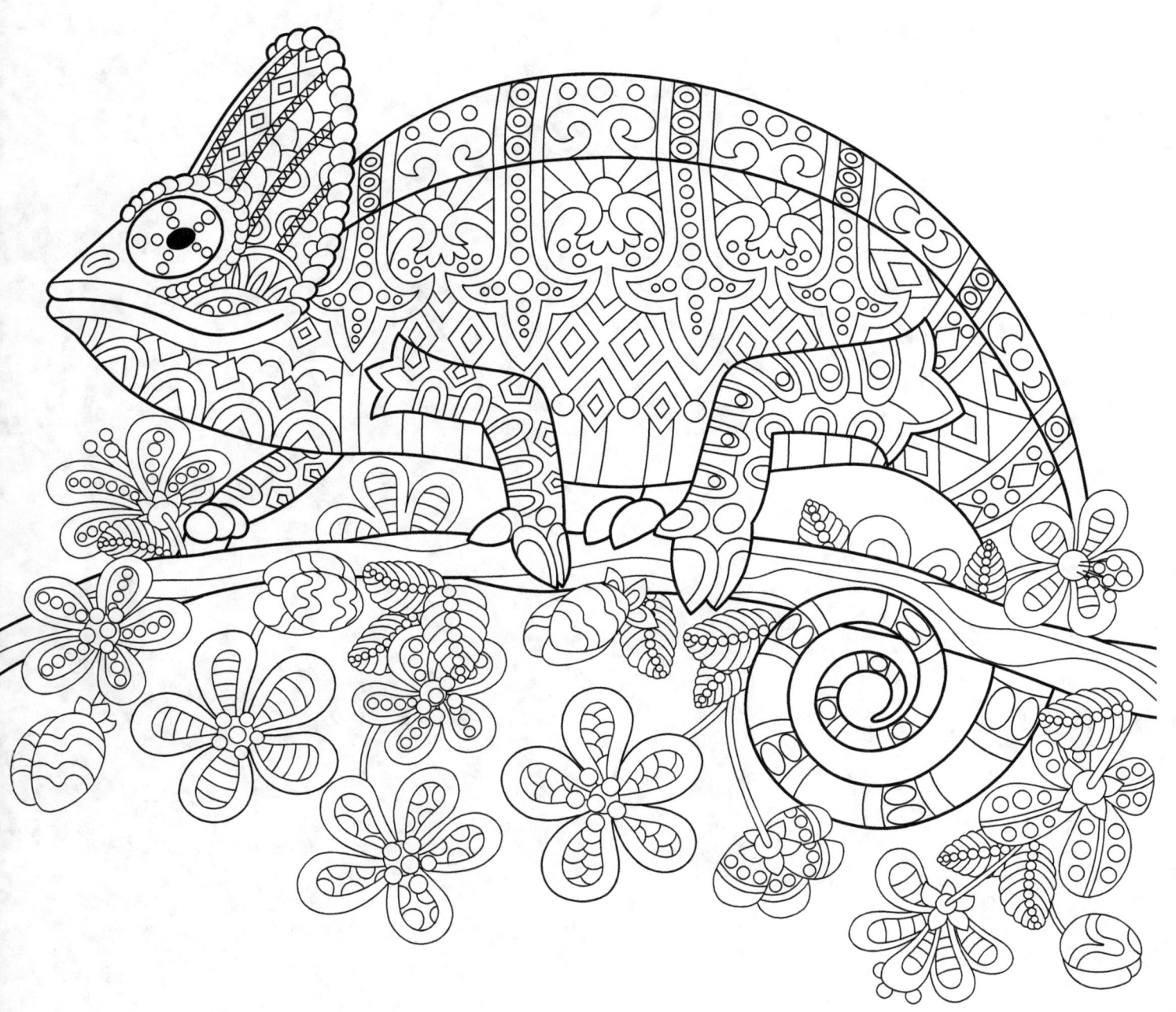

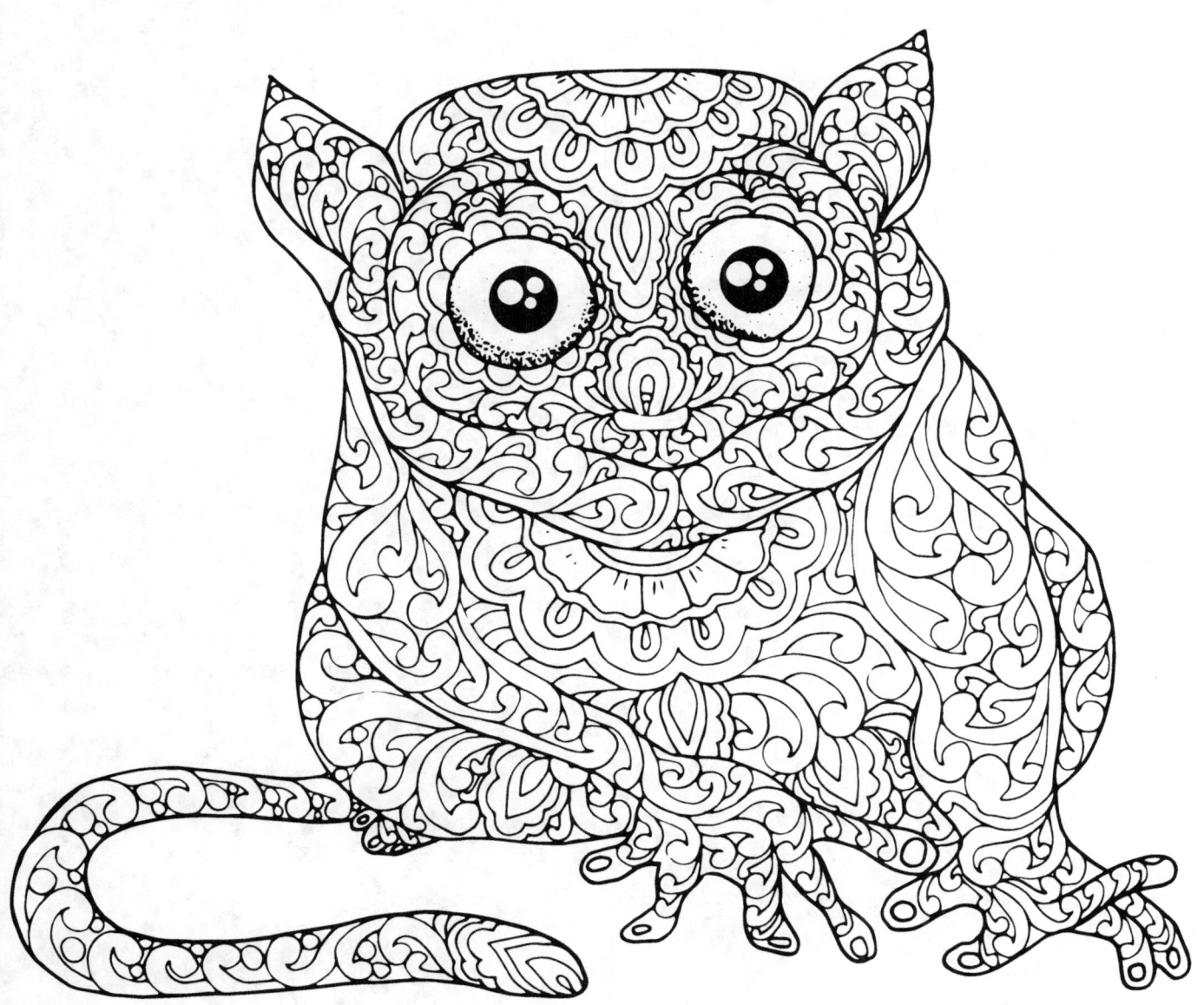

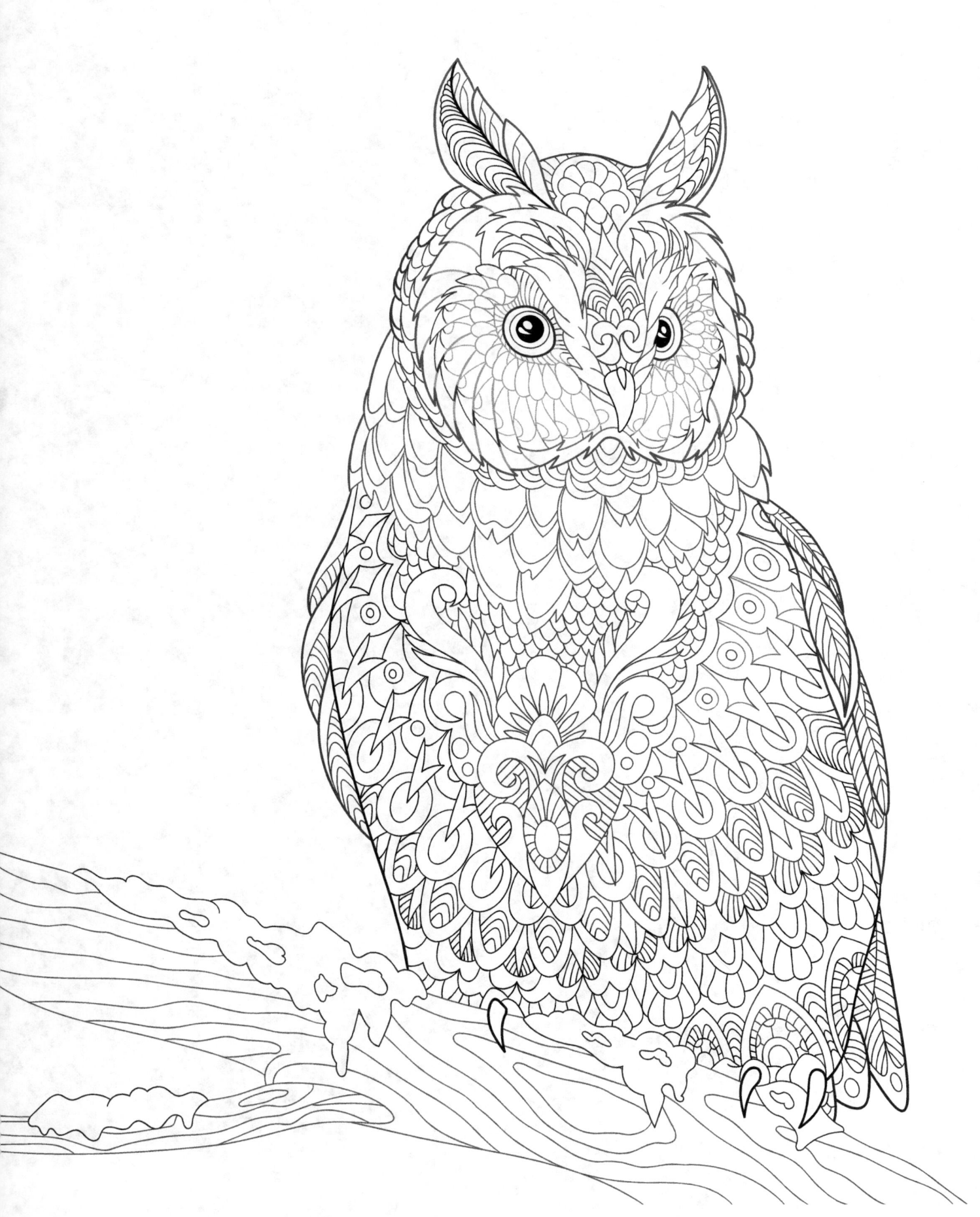

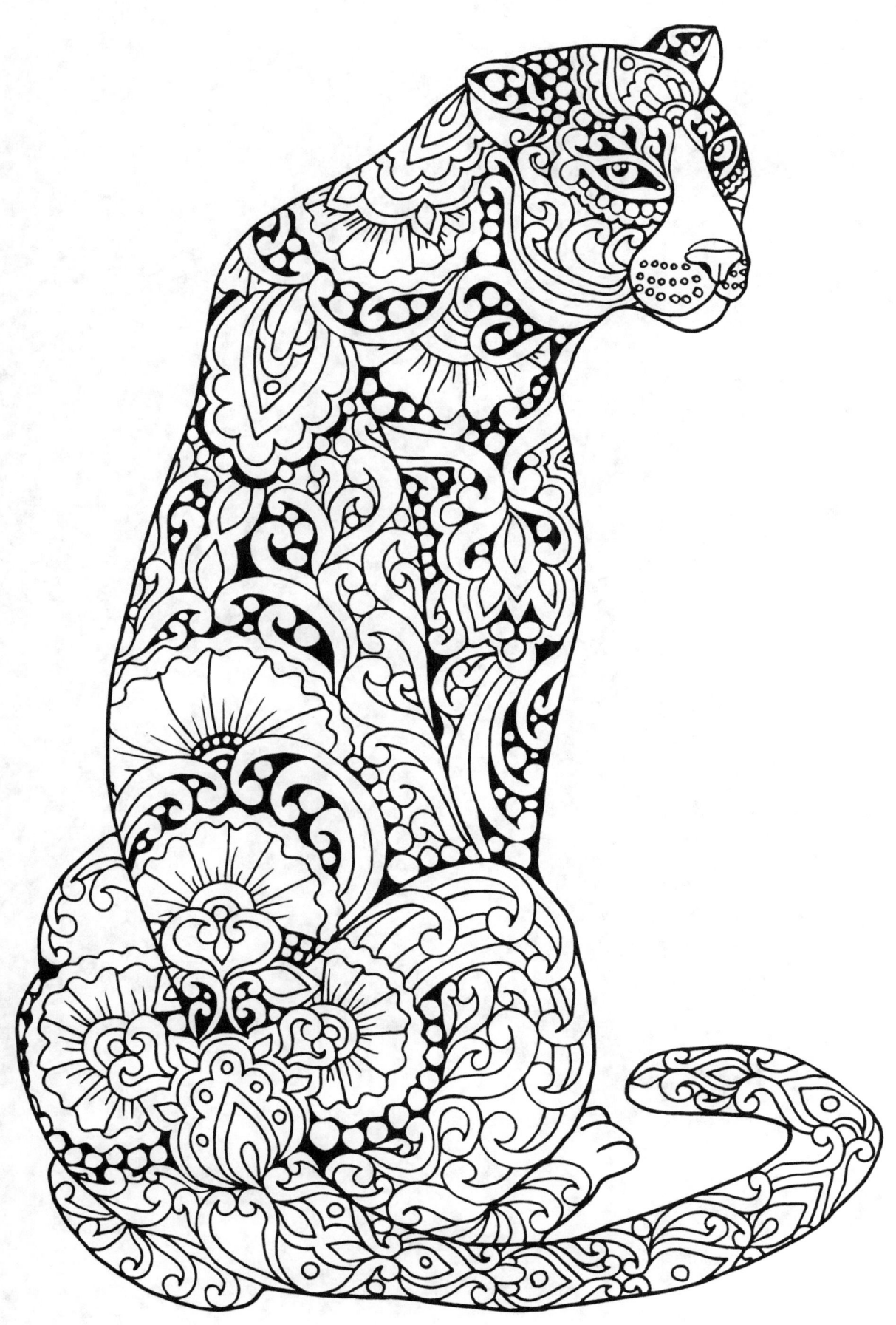

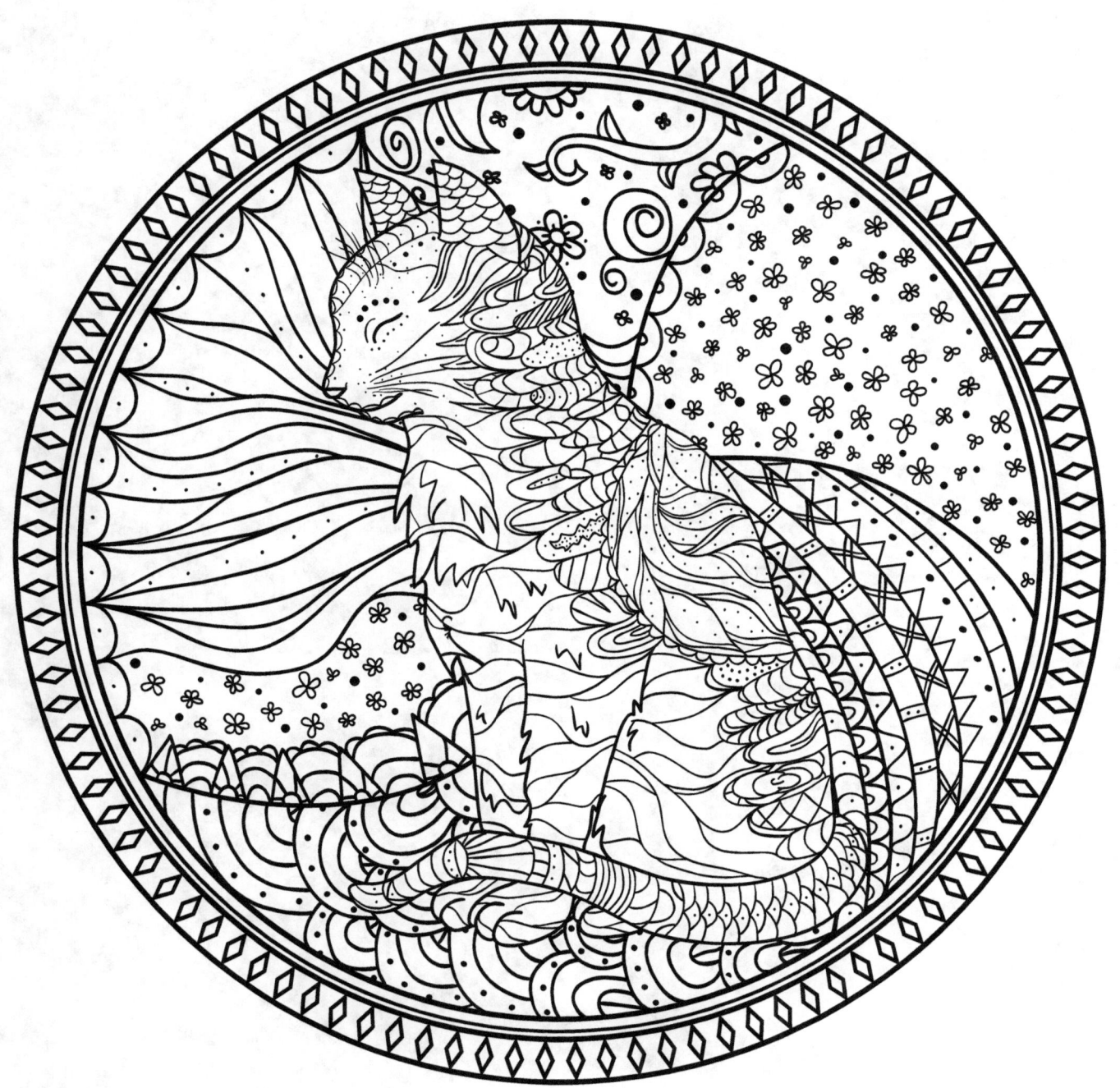

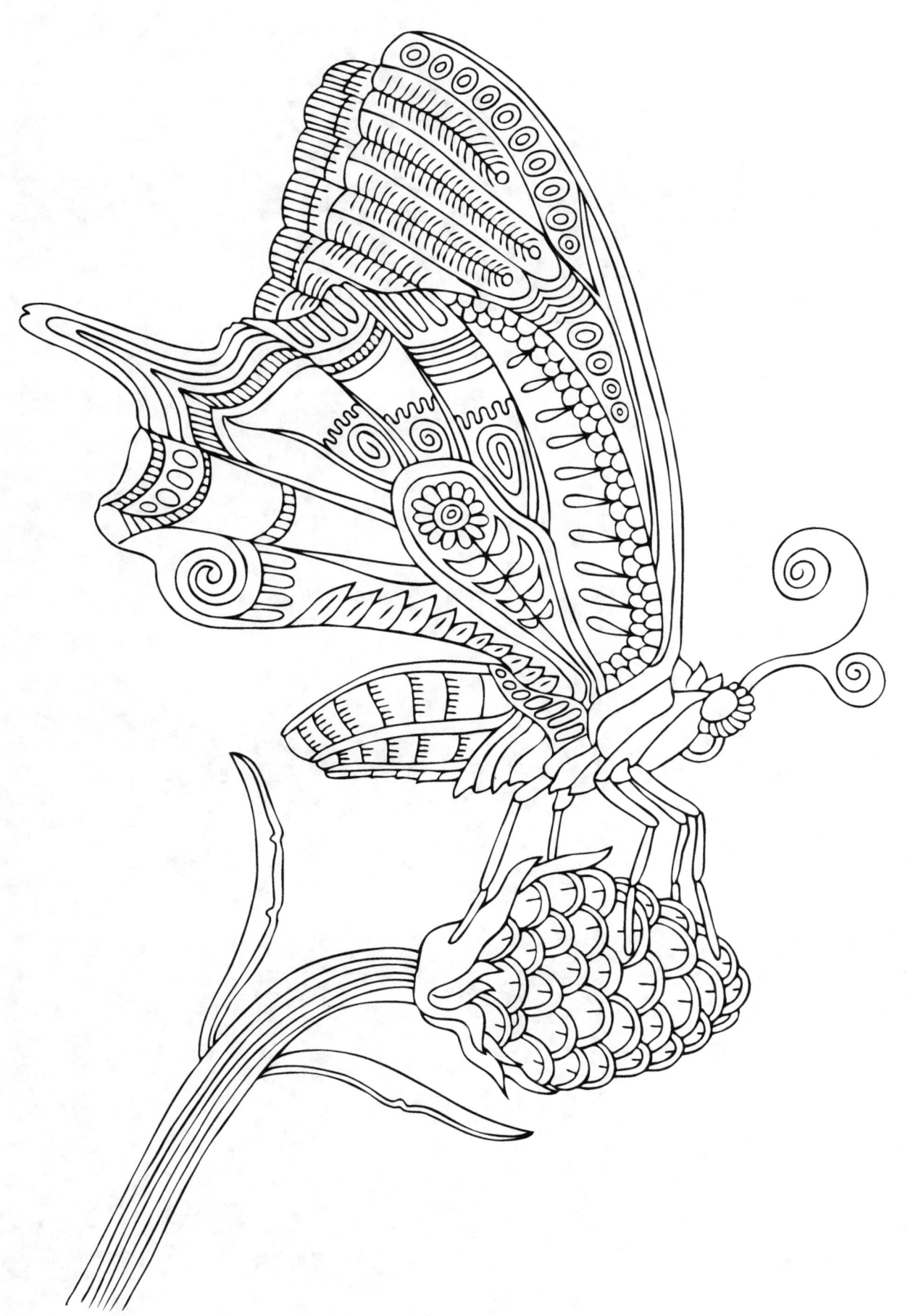

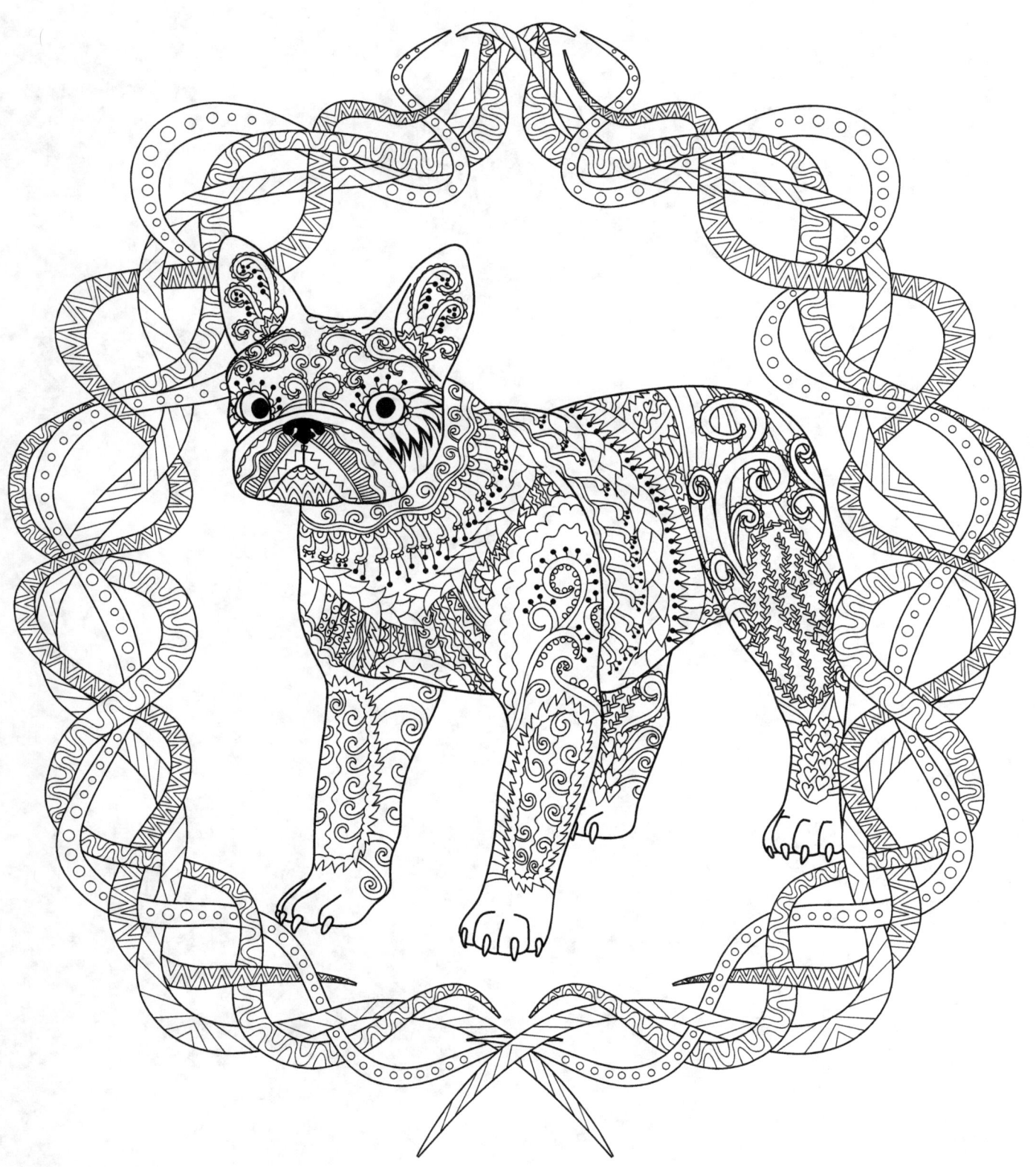

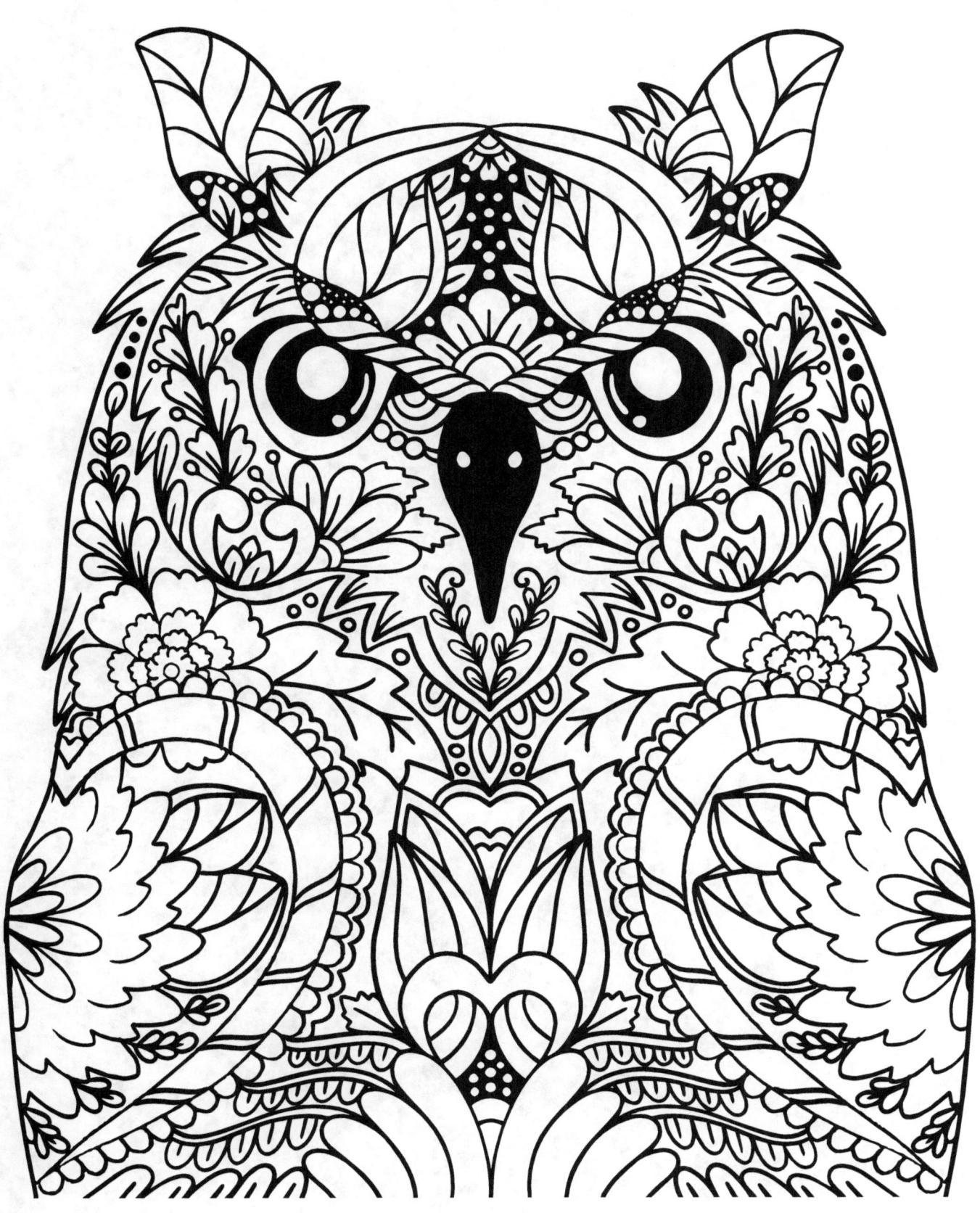

Illustrations réalisées par :

Big Boy
ViSnezh
An Vino
Teamarwen
Natalija Davydova
patrimonio designs ltd
Bimbim
Mika Besfamilnaya
Alexander_P
Nadezhda Molkentin
Alfmaler
Keiti
nichy
Watercolor_bird
Kapom
photo-nuke

www.ingramcontent.com/pod-product-compliance
Lightning Source LLC
Chambersburg PA
CBHW060440220526
45465CB00008B/3212